OUTSOURCING JUSTICE

OUTSOURCING

JUSTICE

The Role of
Nonprofit Caseworkers
in Pretrial Release Programs

Ursula Castellano

FIRST**FORUM**PRESS

A DIVISION OF LYNNE RIENNER PUBLISHERS, INC. • BOULDER & LONDON

Published in the United States of America in 2011 by
FirstForumPress
A division of Lynne Rienner Publishers, Inc.
1800 30th Street, Boulder, Colorado 80301
www.firstforumpress.com

and in the United Kingdom by
FirstForumPress
A division of Lynne Rienner Publishers, Inc.
3 Henrietta Street, Covent Garden, London WC2E 8LU

Library of Congress Cataloging-in-Publication Data
Castellano, Ursula.
  Outsourcing justice: the role of nonprofit caseworkers in pretrial
release programs / Ursula Castellano.
  Includes bibliographical references and index.
  ISBN 978-1-935049-29-6 (hardcover: alk. paper)
1. Pre-trial intervention—United States. 2. Criminal justice, Administration
of—United States. 3. Corrections—Contracting out—United States.
4. Privatization—United States. I. Title.
HV9304.C376 2011
364.6—dc22   2010051305

British Cataloguing in Publication Data
A Cataloguing in Publication record for this book
is available from the British Library.

This book was produced from digital files prepared by the author
using the FirstForumComposer.

Printed and bound in the United States of America

 The paper used in this publication meets the requirements
of the American National Standard for Permanence of
Paper for Printed Library Materials Z39.48-1992.

5 4 3 2 1

To my parents and grandparents

Contents

Acknowledgments

I am grateful to the pretrial release caseworkers, judges, and bail commissioners for allowing me into their organizations. I would also like to thank the defendants and clients who granted me access to their lives through jail interviews and office visits. Many scholars enouraged the genesis and growth of this project. Ryken Grattet once told me that it takes a long time to fully develop ideas. Those words rang true and they motivated me to never give up. Valerie Mendoza, my personal editor, stuck with me through so many chapter drafts. Thank you for helping me to keep writing, Valerie. Completing the final steps of this book would not have been possible without the supportive emails, texts, calls and visits from Marisol Lara and Julie Dummermuth. I am appreciative of the friendship and support of the following people during all stages of this project: Julie Beck, Diane Ciekawy, Anna Maria Marshall, Mary Dias, Drew Hathaway, Susan Miller, Robert Castellano, Haley Duschinski, Colleen Hupke, Chris Dreis, Leon Anderson, Becky Tuttle, and Tom Vander Ven. I would also like to thank Gale Miller and Leslie Paik for their insightful and constructive suggestions for improving the manuscript.

There is a certain culture at the Hall of Justice because everyone knows each other—but to an outsider, the Hall can seem like a strange place. There is an honor or code that drives the relationship between criminal justice and nonprofit workers.

—Superior Court Judge Marconi

1

Outsourcing Justice

Each afternoon at four, the Open Door holds case review meetings, a venue where caseworkers collectively evaluate felony defendants referred by the court for pretrial release services. The program director, Wayne Brooks, invited Judge Nancy Beal to the meeting to learn about treatment options for defendants once they are released from jail. As the meeting commenced, Supervisor Kelsey Martinez tapped at her laptop and the first case was shown through the LCD projector and up on the large white screen. The program status for Laura Polanyi, a twenty-two-year-old Caucasian woman, was labeled "negative termination" meaning she was going to be dropped from the caseload. Kelsey summarized the situation: "Laura was sent over [to the Open Door] from Judge Janice Lee for assessment, a kind of informal diversion. She hasn't been following through on the treatment plan or coming to groups." Judge Beal, who was seated in the back, asked: "Is there nothing more you can do for her?" Kelsey explained, "[Judge Lee] is tough; she [usually] only gives defendants one chance." "Sometimes it takes several chances to get someone to change," Judge Beal responded. Kelsey nodded in agreement to the sentiment but added "it really depends on the judge" in reference to her ability to negotiate greater leniency from the court. Kelsey posed two possible options to her staff: "We can remand her into custody for [drug] detox or set up weekly court dates and give the client a harsh warning." Kelsey tabled the decision when caseworkers could not come to a quick agreement and moved onto the next case.

Kelsey next introduced Robert Gallagher, a thirty-one-year-old Caucasian man. Kelsey explained that his paperwork was sent over to the Open Door by Judge Will Hwang. Caseworker Vince Smith, who interviewed Robert in jail the previous day, summed up the situation. "He has an extensive criminal history. He said he developed mental health issues coming out of the Marines, PTSD [post traumatic stress disorder]. I need to contact MHS [mental health services] for a diagnosis. He's done lots of time, wants a VA [Veteran Administration] pension. He agrees to take meds but balked at going to [counseling] groups. He is homeless and has battery charges. He may be eligible for residential drug treatment." Kelsey added, "We may need to do a second interview to get more information. [Robert] was released through us twice before and terminated negative. There's no plea in the case yet."

William Rand, a forty-six year-old-African American man, was the next case to light the screen. "He was sent over to the Open Door by the courts for an initial assessment," Kelsey narrated. "He left after a few hours and never came back [to the office]. He's paranoid, DD [dually diagnosed with a mental illness and a substance abuse problem] and an alcoholic. He may FTA [fail to appear in court] on Monday. We'll need to do a 'lost and found' [meaning look for him on the streets]. He hangs out around Seventy-seventh and Peachtree in the Northside area. If he reoffends, do we still want him?" The staff agreed to accept him onto the caseload if he attended mental health counseling. The fourth case up for review and discussion was Dalton Smith, a thirty-eight-year-old African American man. "What's going on with him?" Kelsey motioned to Mario Alvarez, his assigned caseworker. "He needs to submit to UAs [urinary analyses] daily and they must be clean." He continued, "If he doesn't go to court on Monday, stay the bench warrant for one day to locate him." Kelsey added, "You know, he's on the drug court waitlist so we will need to make a collaborative decision with [Drug Court] staff [about his treatment plan]."

Towards the end of the meeting, Judge Beal began to inquire about the differences between the Open Door and several of the other jail alternative programs. "Is Pathways looser than Open Door?" she posed the question as if to indicate some prior knowledge. "Yes," Kelsey replied without further comment. Judge Beal and I left the Open Door agency together and walked up to the corner facing the Hall of Justice on a brisk December evening. She remarked positively on the pretrial release options for defendants: "[It's] wonderful because [otherwise] what do you do with people once you let them out of jail?"

***

Reach, Second Chance, Pathways, and Open Door are nonprofit pretrial release programs contracted by the San Miguel County criminal courts to amass comprehensive information about defendants petitioning for release on their own recognizance (ROR).[1] The Reach program processes pretrial release petitions for new felony arrestees. Second Chance provides ROR services to persons arrested on misdemeanor warrants. Pathways is a pretrial release and case management program for homeless defendants charged with misdemeanor offenses. The Open Door is an intensive, supervised pretrial release program for high-risk felony defendants. These four programs represent an expansion of pretrial release services to defendant populations who might otherwise remain in custody due to their social and criminal justice histories.

The case review meeting provides a window into the social worlds of nonprofit pretrial release caseworkers. The original intent of these programs was to offer an alternative to jail for persons who could not afford to buy their freedom. As evident in the vignette, these programs appear to provide a range of services both inside and outside the courtroom. The staff at the Open Door knew a lot about Laura, Robert, William, and Dalton both as potential clients and as criminal cases. In the case review meeting, Kelsey, Vince, and Mario discussed legal tactics to sanction noncompliance and encourage therapeutic options for court-referred persons. Judge Beal's reference to Pathways as "looser" also hinted at diverse program cultures and connections to traditional court functionaries. The structure of the case review also foretold of changing roles beyond the officialdom of the courtroom. At the nonprofit's main office, Kelsey presided over the meeting, and the judge, an audience member, listened to her recommended courses of action.

Pretrial release programs function to ameliorate the monetary discrimination of the bail system and bring equal justice to all defendants pending the adjudication of the criminal charge. Traditionally, a person arrested for an offense secured his or her release from jail by promising to appear in court or depositing valuable property. Eventually, personal bartering arrangements were replaced with contractual business relationships, and in the development of the bail system, defendants posted a cash bond to get out of jail. Those who could afford the financial guarantee were at liberty in the community and those who could not were held to answer. In turn, the monetary emphasis on the bail decision facilitated a private industry to capitalize from the criminal justice process. To broker earnings, the defendant paid a premium usually ten percent of the bail and the bondsman underwrote a surety to the court for the remainder.[2]

Community-based organizations have been at the forefront of overhauling traditional bail practices and institutionalizing pretrial release services into local justice systems.[3] National and state legislation encouraged judges to prioritize nonfinancial release conditions and placed greater emphasis on community supervision to help ensure defendants appeared in court. The San Miguel courts contracted with private, nonprofit organizations to evaluate defendants for release on their own recognizance (OR) independent of other judicial functions. Judges determined that civilian personnel could make a more objective assessment because the criminal justice system is inclined to hold people in custody.[4] Nonprofits are often characterized as principled intermediaries and not unduly influenced by politics, patronage, or profit. While the agencies in this study readily assumed the task of lessening the social and economic inequalities of the legal system they imported values and practices for achieving justice for primarily poor defendants with unforeseen consequences.

Court officials have long relied on outside providers to recommend alternative solutions for crime-related problems, but few studies analyze the role and function of nontraditional actors in criminal case processing. Criminal justice systems are increasingly delegating the task of information gathering and character evaluation to private sector organizations. What kind of justice do nonprofit caseworkers produce and how does it differ from traditional courtroom justice? Do risk assessment and rehabilitative potential take on new meanings when judicial decision making is contracted out to nongovernmental organizations? When justice is for hire, does court officials' legal authority manifest in new ways? This book weaves together several threads to tell a story that is commonly left at the margins of contemporary studies on criminal justice reform. It reveals the practice of law in the private sphere of the nonprofit agency and how the non-legal approaches to problem solving are transported into public courtrooms. Additionally, it maps out the organizational contingencies, ideological compromises, and role conflicts that govern pretrial release decision making at the San Miguel Hall of Justice. I investigate the changing roles of nonprofit pretrial release workers, court officials, and defendants as they navigate this new criminal justice terrain.

Partners in Crime

The book is part of an ongoing dialogue about what happens to publicly funded government services when they are contracted out to private entities, what Crawford refers to as "contractual governance" (2003: 480). This shift of civic responsibility is well documented in the public policy literature (Backer 2005; Boris and Steuerle 2006; Brinkeroff 2002; Salamon 2002; Smith and Lipsky 1993). Salamon (2002) surveys broad scale reorganization of publicly funded services and delegation of civic decision making powers to a private workforce. Smith and Lipsky (1993) refer to nonprofit personnel in the governmental arena as the "new street level bureaucrats" (13) to understand the ways in which they redefine citizen-state relationships through their everyday actions.

As constitutive partners in crime, nonprofits, acting as state sanctioned agents, offer a public sector parallel to private sector outsourcing. Court officials, in collaboration with community-based organizations, address a range of institutional problems such as jail and prison overcrowding, heavy court dockets, and high recidivism rates in order to reduce the ancillary costs associated with traditional prosecutorial justice without committing substantial internal resources (Jurik et al 2000). These partnerships in crime are evident and long standing. Lidz and Walker (1977) trace the origins of therapeutic control to the 1960s national heroin drug crisis which spurred cooperative relationships between clinicians and court personnel to treat nonviolent drug offenders. Miller and Johnson's 2009 book on problem solving courts contextualized the prisoner reentry movement as assisted by "community transition programs" (72) which rely upon local social welfare agencies to provide a diverse range of programmatic services. A centerpiece of California's Department of Corrections and Rehabilitation is community partnerships with corrections to supervise newly released parolees (Backer 2005). Martin Silverstein's (2001) research on Canadian parole hearings observed that outside case managers were taking on the responsibilities of risk management for whole populations of criminal offenders as they transition back into free society.

Criminal justice scholars and practitioners acknowledge the participation of nonlegal actors in both supporting and principal courtroom roles. Importantly, these studies report on the various ways in which they affect the judicial process. In Robert Emerson's (1969) *Judging Delinquents*, the juvenile court clinic was staffed by social workers and child psychiatrists in residency. They typically deferred to the judge's assessment of which cases merited therapeutic intervention however and defined their role as an advisory arm to the court and not as an advocate for treating criminal behavior. In comparison, Seligson (2002) finds in her book, *The Bilingual Courtroom*, that court appointed interpreters affect the evidentiary content of court testimony by using "linguistic alterations" (11) of attorneys' questions and witnesses' responses. Along these lines, there is a small but growing set of literature on treatment professionals in alternative courts and immediate sanctioning programs. The technological surveillance program for domestic violence offenders in Ibarra's (2005) study involved victim assistants and victim advocates some of whom were associated with community organizations for battered women. In a Prop 36 drug treatment program, independent social service providers provided a variety of residential and outpatient services for participating offenders (Burns and Perrot 2008). In Leslie Paik's study of a California juvenile drug court (2006), participating clients were referred to an outside social service program, and substance abuse counselors are active members of the court team and offered in house treatment expertise to court officials. Nolan's book *Reinventing Justice* revealed that treatment providers played a prominent role in the drug court theater (2001). Elsewhere, I investigate how case management professionals, working at the intersections of the social welfare and criminal justice systems, leverage courtroom decision making that results in greater leniency or enhanced punishment for clientele (Castellano In Press).

Most studies of traditional courts however place nonlegal actors at the margins of their investigative focus and at the organizational periphery of the courtroom. *Outsourcing Justice* is centered on the contractual involvement of nonprofit programs and their staff at the pretrial stage of criminal case processing. I explore caseworkers' and court officials' subjectivities, agency cultures, and network ties to understand how they interdependently encumber or unburden who gets out of jail.

Caseworkers in the Courthouse Community

In the *Process is the Punishment* (1979), Feeley observed that the lower courts operated more like marketplaces than rational hierarchical bureaucracies. Rules and procedures were routinely ignored or modified to settle cases quickly. Court officials made deals and cut bargains to reach dispositions in a seemingly haphazard fashion. This study follows in the rich tradition of courtroom studies that seek to understand institutional decision making practices and how organizational actors shape the practice of law (Blumberg 1967b; Cicourel 1995; Eisenstein and Jacob 1977; Emerson 1969; Feeley 1979; Sudnow 1965; Ulmer 1997). Developed in an earlier era, the concept of the courtroom workgroup theorizes that legal actors work collectively with the expressed goal of processing criminal cases quickly and judiciously. Court officials modify their separate powers to dispose of cases by way of informal negotiations and plea bargaining and, consequently, few cases are adjudicated by jury trial (Dixon 1995; Eisenstein and Jacob 1977; Feeley 1979; Lipetz 1984). Eisenstein and Jacob (1977) characterize the workgroup's operation as a balancing act between the goals of individual actors and the collective interests of their sponsoring organizations. As customary to the workgroup, members collectively establish going rates to reflect the group's consensus about what particular crimes are worth in terms of reaching a settlement (Feeley 1979; Sudnow 1965; Walker 2001). In subsequent research, scholars introduced the notion of courts as communities, which pays closer attention to how courtroom cultures constitute the workgroup dynamics (Eisenstein, Flemming and Nardulli 1988; Flemming, Nardulli and Eisenstein 1993; Ulmer 1997).[5] Combined these archetypes of criminal case processing are beneficial for understanding how organizational and political factors influence court officials' adjudicative strategies as well as the meanings they ascribe to legal procedures.

Most of the research on traditional courts presupposes that judges and attorneys are the central actors involved in sentencing decisions. There is less attention paid to the decision making practices at the pretrial release stage of criminal case processing. Demuth (2003) argues that given the substantial amount of discretion available to courtroom actors as well as little oversight, it is important to understand the undercurrents of decision making at this juncture. Throughout this book, I explore how "normal casework" (Jacobs 1990, 101) plays out in ways unique to the cultural context of outsourcing justice to the private sector. In many respects nonprofit caseworkers fulfill a similar function as the "supporting figures" (94) in Feeley's (1979) New Haven court study. These auxiliary personnel, including police officers, clerks, bail bondsmen, bail commissioners, and pretrial service representatives, provided basic information to arrestees; they were responsible for diagnosing and labeling problem cases; and they produced the documents that made up the case file that judges, prosecutors, and defense attorneys relied upon to settle case outcomes. However I show that nonprofit pretrial release workers actively contributed to the workgroup's institutional parameters for judging the worth of a case, and they came to their task with an orientation different than law-trained actors. They were regarded by court officials as trustworthy advisors, and court officials frequently followed along with caseworker recommendations on how to proceed with criminal matters. The data suggest that contract caseworkers accomplished more than gathering and passing on information to the courts; they participate in the formative decision making practices associated with the making of a criminal case. As we will read, pretrial release workers have broadened the scope and depth of their participation in criminal court proceedings beyond the official parameters of their prescribed duties.

Caseworkers' roles and responsibilities in the courtroom workgroup were also facilitated by linkages to their employing agencies. Nonprofit pretrial release programs are semi-autonomous units on par with traditional court officials' sponsoring organizations. The assistant district attorney's willingness to plea bargain on a particular case, for example, is partially informed by the directives and priorities of the Chief Prosecutor. Similarly, while Reach, Second Chance, Pathways, and Open Door must abide by their contractual obligations to the court, they are independent entities governed by a separate board of directors, bylaws, and mission statements. The programs' orientations towards criminal justice issues are related to internal procedures, organizational principles, and interpersonal staff dynamics. Caseworkers and their respective programs, in effect, participate in pretrial release decision making in ways that facilitate and thwart the cooperative goals of traditional court functionaries.

I suggest that contracting pretrial release operations out to the private sector expands our conceptualization of the workgroup in that the numbers, types, and activities of organizational actors involved in routine criminal court processing are more diverse than is commonly acknowledged by scholars and for whom the public is made aware. The network ties between nonprofit caseworkers and court actors further indicate that workgroup dynamics, in space and place, are now mapped out over larger criminal justice topography. Building from Flemming Nardulli and Eisenstein (1993) and Ulmer (1997), I refer to the interagency arrangements between traditional justice actors and nonprofit caseworkers as a courthouse community. The term represents a fuller accounting of the range of stakeholders as well as their sponsoring organizations involved in criminal case processing at the pretrial stage. The notion of a community also represents how outside environmental factors such as mass arrests, budget reductions, and legislative changes impacts pretrial release operations. Courts, as open systems, are made up of loosely coupled yet interdependent units and organizational actors compete for institutional resources and power (Feeley 1979; Hagan, Dewitt and Alwin 1979). Case outcomes are influenced by the ebb and flow of different stakeholders, disparate access to information, and shifts in political capital. The degrees of familiarity and stability among courthouse actors in the community also structure how much power, discretion, and control individuals have to influence case outcomes.[6] The empirical analysis of this book in essence explores what governs judicial processes in a California courthouse when justice is outsourced to nonprofits. The forthcoming chapters reveal that pretrial release practices are not bound by penal statute but are products of how courthouse actors navigate the contested terrain.

Contested Terrain: Risk, Justice, and Power

The book's narrative shows that outsourcing decision making powers to nonprofit organizations and their staffers transforms traditional courtroom justice. First, it culminates as a structural shift in the primary oversight entity at the pretrial decision making stage from the judiciary to the private sector. Second, it reallocates budgetary resources from correctional operations to jail alternative programs. Third, caseworkers' level of participation in criminal case processing brings into view a cultural change in the craft of justice (Flemming Nardulli and Eisenstein 1993). Outsourcing justice involves actors moving institutional values from conventional to alternative approaches to routine casework. The data reveal that what constitutes pretrial courtroom practices however is perilously mapped onto the blurred boundaries between the criminal justice and social justice worlds. I show how these partnerships in crime bring the definitions of risk, justice, and power into a contested sphere.

I explore the way that risk is conceptualized and actualized in the contours of outsourcing justice to private agencies. Caseworkers and court officials labor in what Loseke (2003) calls the "troubled persons industry" (139). The troubled persons in this context are target defendant populations that represent certain social problems, and policies are enacted to address these problems. The primary task of caseworkers and court officials in this study is to negotiate decisions that render defendants eligible or ineligible for pretrial release services. The decision to release an arrestee on his or her own recognizance is a risk-based judgment that the individual will appear in court without monetary bond. Caseworkers' ability to evaluate which defendants are worthy of release stems from court officials' willingness to delegate their authority, yet the mechanisms that make up the court referral and caseworker recommendation reveals varying subjectivities and organizational realities that result in incongruent release decisions and outcomes. Risk decisions on both sides are also products of intuition, opportunism, coercion, and persuasion, similar to the social worlds of sentencing in Ulmer's study (1997). In addition, outsourcing justice results in a transfer of risk; caseworkers are increasingly accountable to the court to demonstrate their competencies as legal actors. Defendants turned nonprofit clients are held personally accountable to outside providers to take responsibility for their actions and demonstrate a willingness to self correct destructive patterns of behavior. Judges who are accountable to public constituents take on occupational and political liability by using jail alternative programs to adjudicate cases. This risk may be enhanced given that court officials are following the counsel of staff persons who are not lawyers or credentialed social service professionals. Courthouse community members adapt to these contingences in creative ways to achieve their goals: they become risk modifiers, risk assessors, and risk takers.

I explore the role of nonprofits in the courthouse community to understand the conflicting perceptions of justice between law-trained actors and caseworkers and how they are negotiated in context. Courts are more than organizational systems that process people through to various institutional outcomes. They represent the basic tenets of American democracy: fairness, due process, and the presumption of innocence. The architects and supporters of pretrial release programs hoped to ameliorate the social and economic inequalities of what Walker calls "checkbook justice" (Walker 1993: 65). Part of the remedy was outsourcing decision making authority to an independent third party for a more impartial and fair handed assessment of a defendant's petition for nonfinancial release. As we will read, a range of pretrial release program services are now fully institutionalized in lieu of bail bonds for many offenses and suspended sentences formerly overseen by probation are replaced with informal diversion sentences under the supervision of these programs. The criteria however that are used by courthouse members to guide jail alternative decisions brings into view larger and more salient questions about the fundamentals of pretrial release. Is it a legal right or a social privilege? What resources are available to caseworkers to help shape what is an inherently judicial determination? Which entity, government or nonprofit, is held accountable for release outcomes? Along these lines, this book also explores the degree to which these agencies surrender their own social justice ideals to participate in contractual governance and, as a counterweight, to what extent they are able to address perceived systemic injustices. In all, the book grapples with how actors achieve justice enhancing practices on the boundary of law and community.

I show how outsourcing justice exercised inverse power differentials and undercut traditional legal procedures. Court officials were less able to move defendants into jail alternative programs short of caseworkers' willingness and capacity to accept them. Staffers' operative powers are enhanced because much of normal casework takes place in the separate private sphere of their nonprofit agencies. Judges and attorneys, however, also adapted to this new playing field to find ways to maneuver and manipulate casework to their own ends. While caseworkers and court officials alike were pressured to succumb to bureaucratic and managerial controls on their decision making they carved out personal autonomy to conspire to a kind of outlaw justice.

They used subservient, discursive, and direct power in particular contexts and catered to certain audiences as a means to make things happen. In Jacobs' (1990) book on the juvenile justice system, probation officers adapted their work practices in ways that enabled them to achieve certain goals in spite of "erratic organizational support" (125). Similarly, nonprofit caseworkers and traditional court officials acclimatized to the organizational ambiguity and altering casts of courtroom actors by tactically vying for influential power. In total, the book documents how outsourcing decision making powers to nonlegal personnel reengineers the structure and function of the lower courts in important ways and results in new institutional roles for caseworkers, defendants, and court officials.

Overview of the Book

The book is organized into three parts. Part one consists of the introductory chapters one, two, and three which chart out the book's theoretical framework, the history and internal organization of the San Miguel courthouse community, and a descriptive account of caseworkers' occupational experiences administering justice. Part two is the ethnographic heart of the book and consists of the empirical chapters four, five, six, and seven and the presentation of the main findings. Part three contains the concluding chapter that summarizes the main findings and offers directions for future research.

Chapter two describes the sociopolitical conditions that created an infrastructure for nonprofit legal advocacy in the San Miguel Hall of Justice, specifically the bail reform movement and the jail overcrowding crisis. I discuss the internal organization of the courthouse community and the primary actors involved in pretrial release practices. I explore the local cultures of nonprofit programs and criminal justice officials and how they cultivate different interagency relationships and reputations. I also map out the general organizational processes that nonprofit caseworkers in partnership with court officials employ to filter cases through the justice system. Chapter three explores how nonprofit agencies afoot in the criminal justice system negotiated surrounding courthouse policies, personalities, and politics to reduce rates of incarceration. In turn, I consider how caseworkers strategically manage their own professionalization in ways that advance their advocacy agenda and elevate their reputational status as agents of the court.

The analytic focus of chapter four draws upon data to illustrate how caseworkers operated at the forefront of the risk assessment stage to conduct character evaluations and assemble evidence of defendants' entitlement to ROR. I highlight the interviewing strategies that screened out problem referrals and provided special advocacy for weak referrals. Caseworkers facilitated interviews in a manner congruent to their commitment to alternative justice and to advocate for jail alternatives which directly benefited defendants who might otherwise remain detained. Defendants' self disclosures however revealed aspects of their lives that caseworkers labeled as evidence they were not amenable to community-based supervision. Chapter five explores the organizational level negotiations and disputes in the courthouse community over the criteria guidelines for judging release eligibility. The data illustrate that courthouse actors relied on various strategies to test the parameters of a good risk beyond the penal statute. The release criteria were also shaped by caseworkers' technologies and methodologies for compiling cases as well as interpersonal relationships with law-trained actors. In addition, nonprofit management scrutinized caseworkers' discretionary power to reject referrals and modified policies that contributed to higher rates of inmates denied entry into the program.

Chapter six highlights how caseworkers expanded their occupational terrain into the early stages of legal adjudication. I primarily focus on the micro level courtroom theater in which caseworkers played the role of assistants to the defense and employed rhetorical strategies to advocate for judicial leniency. I show that caseworkers' legal mediations in the courtroom structured different types of encounters between defendants and traditional court professionals which resulted in alternatives to prosecutorial justice. Chapter seven explores how caseworkers policed defendants' compliance with the terms and conditions of their release. In the courthouse community, caseworkers were the key sanctioning agents and they used the courts as leverage to both motivate and terminate noncompliant clientele. Court officials' emergent treatment authority however often disavowed staffers' recommendations to revoke services for recalcitrant offenders.

In the concluding chapter eight, I surmise that outsourcing justice alters traditional role expectations for caseworkers, legal officials, and defendants. Specifically, I argue that "justice for hire" culminates into new institutional careers for both pretrial release agents and the accused. Caseworkers carried out judging, lawyering, and policing functions. Criminal offenders managed dual statuses as defendants in the courtroom and clients of a nonprofit agency. Judges and attorneys took on roles as treatment facilitators rather than legal arbiters. I propose several avenues for further exploring the emergent role of nonprofit personnel in specialty dockets, including drug and mental health courts.

Lastly, in the method appendix, I discuss how I grappled with my pretrial career as an ethnographer and an unpaid caseworker.

Courthouse Ethnography

This book is based on approximately twenty-four months of ethnographic research with four pretrial release programs in a California criminal justice system. The data are a nexus of participant observation, informal and formal interviews, and archival casework materials. While crafting the research design, the decisive factor that I used to recruit participants was nonprofit organizations that provided contracted pretrial release services for the courts. To collect the data, I spent approximately six months in each program as an observer and unpaid caseworker. This research was collected in two parts. The first stage of the research was conducted in 1998 and 1999. The second stage was conducted between 2002 and 2004. I completed follow up research during the interim period writing the book, including interviews with caseworkers and a judge in 2010.

I independently approached the executive director at each pretrial release agency with a written statement of intent describing the research project, a copy of the interview guide, and the approval letter from the Institutional Review Board (IRB). As a participant observer of pretrial release practices, I sought access to the county jail. The directors of each program sponsored my application for a jail clearance card through the San Miguel sheriff's department. I was required to attend a four hour jail orientation, submit to a background check, and place my fingerprints and photograph on file. I received a laminated I.D. card that included my name, photograph, the date of expiration, and sponsoring organization. I wore the clearance card on my person at all times in order for law enforcement officials to easily identify me as authorized personnel. The clearance card gave me unrestricted access to the processing center in the San Miguel jail as well as nonpublic areas of the courthouse.

Ethnographic research in multiple settings and the collection of multiple forms of data was also done for this book. To capture and record the observational data, I wrote detailed field notes to compile thick descriptions of three organizational settings where the activities of caseworkers took place: the courthouse, the pretrial release agency, and the county jail. These settings are connected to one another in ways that constitute how release decisions are negotiated. During formal courtroom proceedings, I took jottings on the talking strategies that caseworkers and judges used to promote or dispute the defendant's petition for release. I recorded the informal plea discussions between caseworkers, judges, and attorneys in the courthouse corridor. In addition, I observed judges, lawyers, and pretrial release workers engaging in sidebar deliberations and discussing cases in judicial chambers. Ethnography of nontraditional organizational actors in the courtroom contributes to a deeper and more complex understanding of how privatization of criminal justice programs happens on the ground. This methodological approach illustrates the value of "studying up" (judges) (Nadar 1969: 289), studying the middle (caseworkers), and studying down (defendants) to gain a deep understanding of criminal justice processes. At the county jail, I observed caseworkers interview arrestees to assess their eligibility for release. I also spent many hours of participant research doing interviews, completing criminal background checks, preparing court recommendations, observing courtroom negotiations, and attending pretrial conferences in judicial chambers in the course of studying nonprofit caseworkers. I took field notes on how caseworkers worked individually with newly released defendants to help them achieve their treatment goals at the pretrial release agency.

Second, consistent with calls for triangulation of data sources, I completed a total of forty-nine interviews, lasting approximately one hour each, with some interviews lasting as long as two hours with caseworkers, judges, and bail commissioners. I used a semi-structured guide as the primary data collection instrument for conducting the interviews with the research subjects, and I conducted semi-structured interviews with thirty-four caseworkers, three program directors, eight judges, and three bail commissioners. In addition, I interviewed the legal counsel to the sheriff's department about the history of jail overcrowding, pretrial release policies, and the role of nonprofits in the county justice system. I also spoke informally with one female superior court judge about the pretrial release services and their impact on the courts and criminal justice system. This conversation was not included in my interview totals. The third component of this methodology was to collect written records that directly related to defendants' participation in the pretrial release program, including caseworkers' files, court referral slips, and other internal memorandum. In addition, I collected data about the bail reform movement and the subsequent federal consent decree in California to reduce jail overcrowding as well as articles from local newspapers, government documents, and legal journals. I also analyzed the nonprofits' mission statements, organizational brochures, court reports, and other written materials. In total, the research design revealed differences in how legal cases are constructed across multiple institutional settings. These data best identified the features and contingencies of the caseworker's role in the courthouse community.

Throughout the book, I use the acronyms OR (Own Recognizance) and ROR (Release on Own Recognizance) to refer to the judicial decision to discharge a person from custody on their promise to appear to court. I will most commonly refer to nonprofit personnel as caseworkers or staffers. The programs did use local job titles to refer to their occupational roles in the criminal justice system. Reach caseworkers called themselves pretrial investigators. Open Door staffers called themselves court alternative specialists and Pathways personnel referred to themselves as case managers. I will refer to individuals who enter the criminal justice system in terms that reflect the stage of their pretrial process. If, at the point of a referral, the district attorney has not filed criminal charges, he or she is an arrestee. Once the DA files formal charges against the individual his or her status changes to defendant. If the defendant is accepted into the pretrial release program, he or she gains an additional and elevated status of client. The book will also reveal local programmatic terms for individuals at various stages of their pretrial status. For example, Pathways clients who successfully completed their court-ordered treatment and earned a dismissal were called "graduates." Second Chance referrals who failed to comply with program directors were labeled "duds." Open Door defendants who successfully or unsuccessful complied with programmatic expectations were called positive and negative terminations, respectively. The reader should also note that caseworkers often referred to bail commissioners as judges. Finally, I want to note that there were aspects of these programs and their staff that I chose not to disclose for purposes of protecting their identity and their various strategies for achieving tasks that might prove controversial.

---

[1] To protect the identity of the study site, all names, organizations, and locations have assigned pseudonyms.

[2] The bondsmen then act as a third party to help ensure that the defendant appears for court.

[3] The bail reform movement occurred in tandem with a number of historically specific events that advanced the liberties of marginalized social groups, notably the Civil Rights Movement, Johnson's War on Poverty, and the Women's Rights Movement. In 1964, the Department of Justice under President John F. Kennedy and the Vera Institute co-sponsored a national conference to discuss the problems of bail in the criminal justice system, which was widely attended by judges, law enforcement officials, and other court personnel (Thomas 1976).

[4] The source of this datum is a taped interview with San Miguel Superior Court Judge Herbert Mills (a pseudonym).

[5] In collective fashion, work orientations are influenced by shared beliefs among court officials about how to handle criminal cases, their commonly held

values and traditions as well as the special use of language to express ideas (Flemming, Nardulli and Eisenstein 1993).

[6] Prior research noted the degree of stability and familiarly among judges, prosecutors, and defense attorneys in the workgroup were essential for understanding how criminal cases were handled (Eisenstein and Jacob 1977). Workgroup familiarity is generally defined as how well participants know each other and how frequently they interact. The more familiar court officials are with one another, the more likely they are to negotiate case settlements informally, agree about courtroom values and have compatible goals (Eisenstein and Jacob 1977). Workgroup stability refers to how long court officials are assigned to a particular courtroom. In unstable workgroups, judges and attorney rotate in and out of the courtroom on a frequent basis which means that court officials are more likely to rely on formal procedures to settle cases and have lower goal compatibility.

2
Mapping the Pretrial Terrain

"The courts realized during the [jail overcrowding] crisis that they could do something to impact the jail overcrowding. Although there was some resistance to change and some judges felt it was not their job to find a solution, now many judges feel like they do not know what they would do without all the programs."

—Superior Court Judge Herbert Mills

This chapter provides an ethnographic narrative of the San Miguel courthouse community. Specifically, I describe the fieldwork setting and historical context that led up to the institutionalization of four pretrial release programs in the criminal justice system. My purpose in the first section is to contextualize the physical space in which caseworkers conduct their business and the conditions under which the pretrial release programs emerged as well as the function they serve in the jails and the criminal courts. I then turn to an overview of the structures and cultures of the courthouse community members and their sponsoring organizations that are involved in pretrial decision making. In the final section, I map out the possible trajectories for getting out of jail to highlight the roles and responsibilities of nonprofit caseworkers in relationship to traditional justice actors.

San Miguel Hall of Justice: Setting and Context

This study is located in San Miguel County, a large metropolis in the state of California. According to the 2008 U.S. Census, the county population was approximately 825,000. Situated in a coastal region, the demographics of the area populous are culturally and racially diverse, including a large percentage of immigrant families from Latin America, Mexico, and Southeast Asia. The Hall of Justice is located southwest of the central downtown area and encompasses a city block. Most criminal justice personnel commonly referred to the courthouse as "The Hall." The Hall fronts Miller Avenue, a busy, four lane thoroughfare and bail bond agents, bars, and eateries are located across the street. There are twenty-two courtrooms on three floors. It also houses many of the county's main offices, including the Chief of Police, the Offices of the District Attorney and the Public Defender, a district police station, the criminal courts, Central Warrants Bureau, and the Inspectors Bureau. Walking up the wide set of steps towards the front door of The Hall before the nine am court session, there is typically a long line of defendants, family members, and public citizens to pass through the metal detector and show photo identification to the sheriff's deputies stationed at the security portal. Lawyers, judges, court personnel, and nonprofit caseworkers are afforded special classification cards that allow them to bypass the line and enter The Hall through a side gate.

The county jail system is comprised of seven facilities and houses a daily population of 2200 prisoners including new arrestees, probationers and parolees, federal inmates pending transfer, and persons arrested on immigration holds. Four of the jails are located in or adjacent to the Hall of Justice. There is a custody ward at the county hospital and two other jails are located ten miles north of San Miguel. In the Hall of Justice, Jail A and Jail B are located on the fourth and fifth floors above the criminal courts. In the 1990s, San Miguel built a new jail facility adjacent to the Hall, which includes an intake and release facility on the first floor and housing facilities on the upper floors for persons awaiting trial and serving sentences. The newer jail, modeled as a direct supervision facility, is architecturally designed to maximize surveillance and management of the inmate population. The intake center books and processes over 50,000 people annually. The sheriff's deputy station is physically situated in the center of the facility, and the holding cells are positioned along the perimeter. The intended effect allows law enforcement to monitor constantly inmate activity and immediately quell any incidents that threaten the safety of the institution.

In the housing facilities on the upper floors, twenty to forty inmates are detained in separate and self-contained units called pods. A small number of correction officers are assigned to supervise activity, control the entry and exit doors, as well as communicate with the rest of the jail. Some inmates participate in reentry programming such as adult education and alcohol and drug abuse counseling. County jails A and B are commonly referred to as the "old jail." Once you exit the elevator on the fourth floor, to the right, down a long corridor, inmates are detained in prototypical jail cells with steel bars and furnished with bunk beds, stainless steel lavatories, and commodes all bolted to the floor. The women's jail is located to the left of the elevator and cell units are significantly smaller (four to six women per cell). The sheriff's control and command room was also located on the fourth floor.

History of Pretrial Release Programs

Caleb Foote's (1954) pioneering study of the bail system in Chicago exposed the vast disparity between laws on the books and the law in practice with regard to who was held to answer pending adjudication of the criminal charge (Beeley 1966; Dill 1972; Goldfarb 1965; Thomas 1976; Wice 1974). Although a defendant is legally innocent until proven guilty in a court of law, unless the defendant posted bail, they often remained incarcerated until they went to court--or longer-- depending on the seriousness of the charge (Goldfarb 1965; Thomas 1976; Wice 1974). Pretrial detention is, in effect, punishment before conviction and has both immediate and long-range effects on the criminal case. Detainment threatens a person's employment and housing status, disrupts family obligations, and stigmatizes his or her character[1] (Feeley 1979; Irwin 1985; LaFree 1985). Defendants in custody are also more likely to be convicted and with harsher sentences than persons at liberty who are better able to assist in their defense (Feeley 1979; Flemming 1982; Foote 1954; Goldkamp 1979).[2] And so, whether or not to keep an arrestee in jail is one of the most important decisions in the criminal justice process. "The decisions that are made up front, releasing somebody or not, dramatically affects the case for its life. I'm not saying right, wrong, good, [or] bad, but those decisions make a difference," voiced Bail Commissioner Stephen Hayes during our interview in his chambers.

Louis Schweitzer, the founder of the Vera Institute of Justice, a nonprofit, was outraged by the huge public expense of detainment and contended that bail practices constituted a basic human injustice. Poverty, he argued, should not be a barrier to exercising one's legal rights under the law and advocated for a rational, unbiased means of assessing a defendant's likelihood of returning to court. In 1961, the Vera Institute sponsored the Manhattan Bail Project, the first pretrial release project, in New York City (Ares, Rankin, and Sturz 1963; Thomas 1976). The Manhattan Bail Project was staffed by New York University law students who interviewed and screened eligible defendants and recommended those most likely to appear in court (Thomas 1976). The project demonstrated that poor, low level defendants could be safely released and expected to comply with court demands without a monetary bond.[3] Between 1962 and 1965, nonprofit and volunteer-run pretrial release programs based on the Vera model were quickly adopted by criminal justice systems across the country, including a number of pilot pretrial release programs in California (Thomas 1976). The 1966 Federal Bail Reform Act designated own recognizance as the preferred method for release in federal cases (Sherwood-Fabre 1987)[4] and, by 1971, thirty-six states followed suit enacting similar statutes (Murphy 1971).

A national survey published by the Pretrial Justice Institute reported that there are approximately 300 pretrial release programs in the United States and they are housed in a number of different agency settings, including nonprofit agencies under government contract, the courts, county sheriff's departments, and probation departments.[5] The review also revealed that there is an increase in the number of programs operated by independent agencies that are housed outside of the court system and sixty percent of programs operate in jails that are at or over capacity. The institutionalization of Reach, Second Chance, Pathways, and Open Door spans a thirty-four year period and stems from the socio-political dynamics of the bail reform movement as well as the jail-overcrowding crisis. In 1964, in the spirit of the bail reform movement, Reach began offering pretrial release services in San Miguel County Jail. Staffed by law students and Vista National Peace Corps volunteers, caseworkers recommended OR releases using a risk assessment point scale to evaluate a defendant's eligibility (e.g. three points for having a job longer than six months and minus one point for a prior conviction), with a specific number of points needed for release. Reach gave priority to persons arrested on felony offenses in part because misdemeanants were more likely to make bail or have their cases dismissed, whereas felons were less likely to afford bail and typically waited longer for their arraignment.[6] During its early tenure, caseworkers were clearly motivated by substantive goals. Kathryn Edwards, then Reach director, asserted that caseworkers attempted to get a favorable ruling from the court. In spite of Reach's early programmatic success, its pretrial release practices came under scrutiny by the legal community when a judge released an arrestee and the individual was later arrested for a violent offense. Court officials determined that judges relied too heavily on the point scale system; as a result, Reach no longer made recommendations and staff were under instructions from the nonprofit's board of directors to exercise no pressure for release.

Many of the changes in American criminal justice policy are linked to the shifting political winds between protecting individual rights and controlling crime. This is true of the bail reform movement as well. The tide turned in favor of law and order policies in the 1970s which re-prioritized public safety over poverty concerns. Subsequent bail reform bills were defeated in the state legislature and increases in crime rates led to public tolerance for institutionalizing preventive detention measures. In 1982, California voters passed Proposition 4, which restricted bail for defendants whom judges determined to pose a public threat. These measures overturned previous state court decisions and procedural amendments awarded to bail reform advocates at earlier stages in the movement. Bail reform advocates experienced an additional setback on the national level when Congress passed the Federal Bail Reform Act of 1984. The legislation empowered federal judges to detain defendants deemed a flight risk or potentially dangerous to public safety (Sherwood-Fabre 1987).

Anti-crime policies negatively impacted county jail populations across the state (Welsh 1995). The San Miguel sheriff's department blamed the overcrowding problem on twelve years of law-and-order legislation that got tough on crime at the state and federal levels and lead to restriction on parole, minimum sentencing laws, local ordinances to reduce street crime, and sentencing enhancements for weapons and use of force (Kelling and Coles 1996; Welsh 1995). The inmate population at San Miguel jail soared because many felony defendants were no longer eligible for OR release. At the time of the jail-overcrowding crisis, Reach was the only pretrial release program in the San Miguel jail for felony defendants. Over the past twenty years changes in the state's penal code and successful lobbying by bail bondsmen increasingly narrowed the eligibility criteria for OR release, particularly for serious offenses.[7] Stacy Abaya, a Reach supervisor, explained to me, "Fifteen years ago we could present persons charged with robbery, domestic violence, and on probation. Now there is a wide range of charges that are no longer eligible."

In 1979, a class action lawsuit was filed on behalf of several San Miguel County Jail inmates in the federal courts citing violations of public safety and health standards due to overcrowding, what Welsh (1995) called the "the trigger stage" (24) that prompted a legal response to the problem of jail overcrowding. The lawsuit culminated in a consent decree that laid the groundwork for the political and social dynamics that helped to formulate an emergent criminal justice policy in the wake of the institutional crisis (Welsh 1995). When the county sheriff's department failed to comply with the mandate, it accrued million of dollars in court contempt fees. Part of the jail's function is to move inmates back out onto the streets as quickly and efficiently as possible, yet many inmates failed to meet the increasingly restrictive OR criteria and could ill afford to post bail. Short-term solutions were invented to comply with the court order including evicting federal inmates, double-bunking cells, and renting jail beds from a neighboring county. Judge Richard Kwan explained to me during an interview in his chambers that in order to positively impact the jail population: "Judges need to release as many people as they can, not just those that [fit] the legal criteria." The federal judge overseeing the consent decree directed that the fine monies be used to expand pretrial release programs to reduce the monetary discrimination inherent in the bail bond system and help ease jail crowding.

One of the target jail populations for OR release was misdemeanants arrested on bench warrants, a population of defendants previously ineligible because they had a history of failing to comply with court demands. In 1959, a legal statute was enacted that allowed for most non-violent misdemeanants to be cited (released without a judge's approval) out of jail. The citation law was on the books, but the police, who then managed the jail operations, relied on various legal loopholes to keep people behind bars. For example, the police refused to cite out a defendant if he or she did not have a local address. In the 1970s, the sheriff's department assumed responsibility for the booking process in the jail and applied the citation law more liberally as a mechanism to reduce jail overcrowding. However, there were limitations to the legal statute: sheriff's deputies were not empowered to cite out misdemeanor defendants arrested on bench warrants. Second Chance was contracted to offer pretrial release services to this group as a temporary solution to overcrowding, yet when the consent decree was settled the program was retained in order for the court to get information on misdemeanor warrants.

Law enforcement officers hoped the new jail would remedy the overcrowding program, but in the mid-1990s, San Miguel County was once again facing congested jail cells along with high recidivism rates. The San Miguel Sheriff's department further expanded ROR services to include chronic homeless offenders. Homeless persons are generally considered poor candidates for pretrial release due to their transient existence and because they often have long histories of failing to comply with court orders. This population has a high percentage of contacts with the criminal justice system because they participate in routine activities that expose them to public scrutiny and increase the likelihood of arrest (Snow, Baker, and Anderson 1989). The adoption of anti-panhandling laws and other ordinances to reduce street crime (Kelling and Coles 1996) also galvanized the policing of quality-of-life crimes, which resulted in high numbers of arrests for public drunkenness, disturbing the peace, illegal lodging, and urinating in the street. Pathways was adopted into the jail system to provide intensive community-based supervision to homeless persons charged with low level offenses.[8]

Chronic felony offenders were another target population for OR release to ameliorate overpopulated jails. Many of those charged with serious felony offenses or who have long histories of arrests and convictions are considered too risky for pretrial release without extensive supervision (Austin, Krisberg, and Litsky 1985). Consequently, this defendant population remained in custody pending disposition of their case which contributed to the ongoing jail crowding crisis. Criminal justice reformers in support of overhauling the bail system argued that preventive detention laws contributed to the problem. Supervised pretrial release (SPR) programs were implemented into criminal justice systems nationwide as a response to both sides of the bail reform debate. The Open Door now contracts with the courts to operate an intensive case management program for felony defendants who are ineligible for release through Reach.

At the time of this research, the four programs operated full time in the San Miguel Hall of Justice. These long standing partnerships between nonprofit agencies and the courts reflects a realization that government actors are less able to respond effectively to the crime problem and rely on outside human service providers to evaluate, treat, and control a range of defendant populations.

Internal Organization of the San Miguel Criminal Courthouse Community

I now turn to an overview of the primary courthouse actors involved in pretrial release practices and describe the cultural and structural factors that shape their orientation towards legal decision making. I also consider the social and institutional dynamics that govern relationships between caseworkers, bail commissioners, superior court judges, state attorneys, and law enforcement officers.

Pretrial Release Programs and Their Staff

Reach, Second Chance, Pathways, and Open Door are private 501 (c) (3) nonprofit organizations and they all operate on the same core operating principle: to evaluate defendants for OR release in lieu of bail. Caseworkers fulfill similar functions of interviewing defendants in jail; compiling an OR case with the necessary forms, references, and documentation; presenting cases to a judicial authority; and supervising newly-released defendants to ensure they return to court. The programs do differ in important ways: staff size, clientele, organizational ideology, and network ties with court officials. My goal here is to orient the reader to the pretrial release agencies as sponsoring organizations in terms of how they perform tasks and govern the actions of staff members. I will delve deeper into caseworkers' occupational backgrounds, aspirations, and on-the-job challenges in chapter three.

Reach: Felony Arrestees

Reach provides twenty-four hour pretrial release services to new felony arrestees whose eligibility is determined by penal statute. At the time of the Reach interview, the majority of persons had not yet been formally charged with a crime by the district attorney's office. The staff processes an average of 1200 cases per month. The nonprofit is staffed by a program director, four supervisors, and eleven part-time and full-time caseworkers.[9] Reach staffers were generally in their twenties and thirties; about one half of the staff were in college, had some college or held a college degree. One Reach employee resigned from her job as a caseworker to become a probation officer. No other caseworkers in the study aimed for occupational advancement in the criminal justice labor force. Caseworkers operated in three eight-hour shifts: day, swing, and graveyard. They spent the majority of their time in their satellite office in the jail's processing center conducting interviews and in the main office finalizing case preparations. The supervisors usually worked in the main office summarizing rap sheets and making court reminder calls. Staff members delivered OR cases to the bail commissioners and picked up police reports on an as-needed basis.

The interactions between Reach management and staff were friendly and informal. Each day around noon, the day shift staff and the director sat down to have lunch together. The office was located across the street from The Hall, on the fifth floor of an old narrow building. The space was comprised of a tiny lobby, a common work area with desks and computers, and a break room. The break room was cozy, furnished with a small conference table and folding chairs, a mini refrigerator, and a microwave. The only window looked out onto busy Miller Avenue at the county courthouse. A large corkboard is pinned with advertisements, employee memos, and the weekly work schedule. A time clock is fastened to the wall in the far corner and time sheets are filed in a haphazard fashion. Down a narrow hallway, two more offices served as the director's office and a storage area. The office was busy in the morning and the phone rang continuously until around two in the afternoon when it quieted down. The Reach office had few visitors but on occasion attorneys, defendants, or family members dropped by to request services.

Caseworkers' screening practices are bureaucratically organized to help them work efficiently and minimize mistakes. Since the program does not make recommendations as to the merits of the defendant's petition for pretrial release, the staff is primarily concerned with whether the case contains accurate, complete, and objective information to the court. They adopted a self-proclaimed neutral role as information gatherers. Stacy said with resignation, "I leave it up to the documents." Bridget Milne, a part-time worker, explained, "If somebody gets out and they end up doing something bad, it could come back to you. I'm just a layperson. If it's up to a judge to make the decision, they have more authority than me. Who am I to be letting people out [of jail]?" In spite of their long hours and heavy caseload, only an average of twenty five percent of defendants was granted pretrial release on a given day. Reach however participated in the creation of pretrial release petitions in ways that were advantageous and detrimental to the defendant's chances of getting out of jail. The small percentage of releases can be partially explained by the serious charges levied against the defendants but it was also attributable to Reach's technical methods for compiling cases and weak social ties to the bail commissioners.

Second Chance: Misdemeanor Bench Warrants

Second Chance provides pretrial release services to misdemeanor warrants. The program is staffed by a director and four part-time caseworkers. Second Chance caseworkers were in their mid-twenties— in college or just out of college. Some staffers were taking a few years off before going to law school or a postgraduate degree program.[10] Caseworkers screened a monthly average of 250 referrals and approximately forty-five percent were deemed legally eligible for release although a smaller percentage was presented for release because they lacked community ties, a stable address, or a good reason for missing court. The defendants were most commonly facing charges for suspended license, burglary, theft, drug possession, prostitution, assault, and vandalism. The program is housed in the jail's processing center and staff occupied a small office next to Reach; the office was glass partitioned and sparsely furnished. There was a gray, institutional-looking metal desk and two chairs for the caseworker and the defendant to use during interviews and a tall filing cabinet.

The ideological mission of the nonprofit is what the director called "strictly advocacy." Caseworkers recommended releases to bail commissioners in chambers and an average of ninety percent of petitioners were granted release. Staffers felt strongly that their role was to advocate for individual defendants as well as social change throughout the judicial system. The staff was actively involved in writing reports on patterns of racial inequality in police arrests and investigating incidents of illegal detainments to affect institutional reform.

Pathways: Homeless Misdemeanors

The Pathways program provided supervised release to homeless misdemeanants facing low level charges and short jail terms. Once the defendant was out of jail, employees worked closely with judges and public defenders in the five misdemeanor courtrooms to divert offenders from prosecutorial justice by proposing treatment alternatives in the community. The program provides services to an average of one hundred clients each year. The program is staffed by the program director and three full-time caseworkers. Pathways caseworkers were all college educated, the majority were in their late twenties and thirties and committed to working in the social services field.[11] The clientele were typically arrested for petty theft, assault, disorderly lodging, trespassing, and drug-related offenses. Caseworkers usually spent the morning hours (typically nine to twelve) in the courtroom delivering reports, meeting with new clients, and talking with judges and attorneys about pending cases. They spent much of their time outside the courtroom working with clients in shelters, encampments, SRO hotels, and on street corners to help "improve their quality of life" as one staff person put it. Caseworkers frequently accompanied clients to doctor appointments, to the DMV to get an identification card, or to the Veteran's administration to inquire about benefits eligibility.

The Pathways office was located on Sixteenth Avenue, a ten minute walk from The Hall in a basement unit of an old-residence-turned-commercial building. At the office, homeless clients were invited to drop in without an appointment. Caseworkers provide food, clothing, temporary storage, the use of the phone, and the office safe for holding cash. Clients slept on the couch or milled around outside smoking cigarettes. A sign on the office wall allotted each client five cigarettes a day. The office included a kitchenette, a bathroom, a reception area, and a separate work room with a desk, computer, filing cabinets, and chairs. The supervisor's desk showcased the small gifts that clients brought her, including a small mirror and a china teacup. If not in court, caseworkers spent a typical morning at the office holding case review meetings, preparing court reports, and readying supplies. It was relatively quiet until 11:30 neared when the office accepted clients. Around that time, there was knocking on the door which caseworkers sometimes chose to ignore: Staffer Manuela Vega said to me shaking her head, "Clients know the office isn't open yet." By 11:30, the knocks and bangs became more frequent and louder until the door opened. The homeless program is based on a harm reduction model, which means that staffers' approach to casework is to "meet clients where they are" rather than imposing specific treatment goals. Caseworkers recognized compliance in nontraditional ways, such as reducing drug and alcohol use as opposed to complete abstinence.

Open Door: High Risk Felony Defendants
Open Door is an intensive, supervised pretrial release program for felony defendants charged with serious offenses and who have long histories of criminal justice contacts. The program is staffed by a program director, three supervisors, and six caseworkers. Open Door caseworkers were in their thirties and forties and a smaller percentage of people held college degrees; one caseworker held a Masters in Social Work (MWS). Many staffers in this agency had previously worked in human services, such as homeless shelters and drug rehabilitation centers.[12] The supervisors primarily worked in the twelve felony courtrooms presenting progress reports, discussing cases with judges and attorneys, and picking up new referrals. The referrals were handed over to caseworkers who were responsible for conducting jail interviews. Caseworkers typically conducted two to three interviews a day and then returned to the office to prepare release recommendation reports for the court and to meet with drop-in clientele.

The Open Door is situated on Ninth Avenue, across the street and around the corner from The Hall. The agency was housed in a two story building of no architectural significance. Beyond the reception area, small offices lined up along the right side and there were two large open spaces with cubicles. The program director described the Open Door as a "triage center" because the casework activity was driven by crises. "Sometimes it is really busy and sometimes there is lots of downtime," he said. My experience with the office environment matched this depiction. The office was often abuzz with people and activities. Clients frequented the agency to check in with caseworkers, attorneys came by to drop off paperwork and inquire about their clients. Newly released inmates were brought over to the office for program orientation.

The agency was founded on progressive political values and a commitment to grassroots legal reform. The nonprofit aimed to improve its professional presence in the courts and management introduced the mantra of accountability to the staff which prioritized streamlining casework practices and clearing the [criminal] cases from the court calendar quickly. In contrast to Pathways, the culture of casework practices at the Open Door was "tough love" similar to Burns and Peyrot's (2003) study on California drug courts. The tough love approach subjected the clients to strict program rules, such as checking in regularly, participating in prescribed rehabilitation programming, and passing random drug tests.

Courtroom Judges

There is a long-standing practice among judges to confine persons determined to be dangerous or high risk. Judges rely heavily on legal criteria (Gottfredson and Gottfredson 1988) (i.e. prior criminal record and criminal charge) but release decisions are negatively influenced by police officers' written remarks on the offender's appearance and demeanor at the time of arrest (Allen 1959; AFSC 1971; Walker 1993). Judges considered other factors such as community ties and employment status (Petee 1994; Walker 1993) yet the subjective nature of extra legal criteria disproportionately screened out defendants who were meant to benefit from the nonfinancial release option. Release decisions were vulnerable to court officials' prejudicial view which correlated with the petitioner's class, race, and gender status. Demuth (2003) found that Hispanic defendants faced a "triple disadvantage" (899). In comparison to Caucasian and African American defendants, they were more likely to be denied bail, have the highest bail, and they were least able to afford bail to secure their release. They were also the least likely group be to granted ROR by the court. In working closely with caseworkers and their respective programs, however, judges articulated and I observed that they were more willing to release defendants. Newly elected Judge Linda Delaney suggested that caseworkers' routine involvement in the courts introduced a different way of looking at cases in contrast to the practice of common law. She said during an interview, "Generally judges are pretty conservative because they operate on precedent and things like status quo. These programs go against that kind of thinking." Many judges, but certainly not all, were interested in alternative-to-traditional forms of justice for chronic offenders.

It behooved caseworkers to be aware of shifts in the court's political and organizational landscape. In 1998, California voters passed a constitutional amendment to unify the misdemeanor and superior courts into a single court trial system. The judges in this study are now operating under the single title of Superior Court Judge. The general drive towards unification was to reduce duplication and ineffective use of judges and staffing of the two court system.[13] It also impacted the routine practices of pretrial release workers albeit in small ways. For example, Second Chance and Reach explained that, after unification, some judges who enjoyed their newly elevated status refused to sign pretrial release approval forms if the paperwork still read "municipal court judge." Stacy recalled, "One [judge] said that he wanted to forget about [OR releases] tonight because I'm sick of crossing out municipal courts." Other judges scratched out the old title and reprinted superior court judge prior to signing it.

Judges' rotating courtroom assignments was also a meaningful event for caseworkers' ability to advocate for alternative justice. One day in case review, Lee Mitchell, an Open Door Supervisor, announced the new court assignments starting that Friday. He said, "The first floor judges are all really good, old pros and they want more information about the client... most of the judges on the bench have been appointed by (Republication governors) Davis and Wilson and not one had a criminal defense background." In chapter one, Kelsey Martinez explained that her options for dealing with Laura's case, "really depend[ed] on the judge" because they differed in their willingness to work with caseworkers and accommodate their treatment recommendations. As we will read in the forthcoming chapters, caseworkers see it to their advantage to be aware of judges' idiosyncrasies, their judging style, and their conscription to formal law and willingness to consider treatment alternatives. Open Door staffers, for example, claimed Judge Janice Lee would not release persons charged with felony drug-selling offenses, and Second Chance staffers had less success convincing Bail Commissioners Paul Krupky and Steven Hayes to release misdemeanors with multiple cases involving driving with a suspended licenses.

Bail Commissioners

Feeley (1979) identified bail commissioners as one of the supporting pretrial release specialists in the New Haven courthouse yet little is known about their role and function in criminal case processing. Previously, courtroom judges were assigned to review pretrial release petitions twice a year for one week on a rotating basis in addition to managing their court calendar. Due to judges' disparate release decisions, the judiciary began to question the efficacy of this systemic practice. A primary concern was that judges' demanding court calendars did not allow them enough time to read the whole case. It also did not allow for a feedback loop meaning that judges did not know if they had made good release decisions: Did the defendant come back to court? Was he or she re-arrested on a new criminal charge? In place of the rotation system, court officials created the bail commissioner position to ensure consistent and uniform pretrial release decisions for misdemeanor and felony arrestees petitioning for pretrial release as well as to relieve the responsibility from superior court judges who were often overburdened with full dockets.

Bail commissioners did not enjoy the same levels of judicial authority as courtroom judges but they were responsible for making some of the first, and most important, judicial decisions about criminal cases. In particular, they granted and denied all OR petitions for the Reach and Second Chance programs. Bail commissioners were appointed by the court and they tended to keep their assignments for several years; they often aspired to be elected or promoted to a courtroom judge.[14] The majority of past and present bail commissioners came from legal defense backgrounds. One might surmise that this would tend to make them more sympathetic toward defendants and grant more releases. Yet in an interview, Bail Commissioner Krupky said that he was surprised at his willingness to keep people in jail in spite of his background in criminal defense work. He said during an interview with me, "I assumed I would be more lenient."

Bail commissioners' release decisions for felony defendants in particular were informed by their position relative to other powerful institutional actors that had a stake in the release outcome. Superior court judges closely monitored bail commissioners' release decisions. Judge Kwan was the first person to hold the bail commissioner position. During an interview, he recalled, "When I first started, it was a new system and [superior court] judges didn't like it. At one point, judges were remanding people that I was releasing." Other bail commissioners experienced similar types of institutional controls over their release decisions. In an interview, Bail Commissioner Krupky noted that if he made a "mistake" and released a defendant thought to be inappropriate, a courtroom judge "would let him know" with a phone call. Similarly, Bail Commissioner Delaney said to me that she often "sought out advice on whether or not to release a defendant" from a more experienced judge. And so, early on, bail commissioners were pressured to make pretrial release decisions that followed judicial precedent. Reach caseworkers, conscious of this social dynamic, derided the bail commissioners' tendency to look for approval from courtroom judges by saying that they are not able to "defend their own decisions." Beyond the politics of the judicial hierarchy, however bail commissioners' routine release decisions were informed primarily by legal and extra legal criteria.

Prosecutors and Defenders

San Miguel county prosecutors and public defenders are involved in OR cases to varying extents. State attorneys had little or no contact with Second Chance staffers, and public defenders were actively involved with Pathways, Open Door, and Reach caseworkers to help get their clients out of jail and prepare a legal defense. District attorneys negotiated prosecutorial alternatives with Pathways and Open Door staff usually in the formal capacity of the courtroom or less formally in the judge's chambers.

The historical disparities in organizational resources and grant funding for state attorneys may partially explain the more significant relationships between public defenders and caseworkers. The resources afforded to the Office of the Public Defender are considerably less than those provided to the District Attorney (Uphoff 1992). According to the county controller's office, San Miguel's public defenders handle a heavy caseload exceeding 200 felony cases and 600 misdemeanor cases, which surpasses the American Bar Association's standard of 150 felony and 400 misdemeanor cases. In Davis' (2007) book *Arbitrary Justice*, she observed that the district attorney holds discretionary powers to pursue or dismiss criminal charges while the public defender is less able to control the number of cases that are assigned by the court.

Uphoff (1992) refers to defense attorneys as beleaguered dealers because they often have constrained resources to mount a defense. The District Attorney's office is also better equipped to successfully prosecute defendants due to the investigatory powers of the police force, a crime lab, and the medical examiners unit at their disposal. Defenders then appreciate caseworkers' commitment to their client's welfare and their assistance in helping to impact positively the case disposition. Caseworkers keep track of the client and make sure that they attend all of their court dates. At times, caseworkers armed the public defender with privileged client information before reporting it to the judge to help leverage the defense. Caseworkers, however, voiced concern that public defenders took advantage of their programs as a way to reduce their caseloads. For example, staffers claimed that public defenders shopped their clients around and made referrals to multiple programs to get their client out of jail, what caseworkers called "double dipping."

For many public defenders, however, referring a client to pretrial release programs is a last resort. As the legal advocate, the attorney wants to get his or her client out of jail under the least restrictive conditions. At the initial hearing, they make a motion to the court to grant the defendant unsupervised release on their own recognizance or a nominal bail bond. Depending on the nature and seriousness of the charge, the public defender may also try to settle the case quickly with the prosecutor during a pretrial conference. Referring more difficult defendants to Open Door or Pathways may get their client out of jail but it takes several days for the caseworker to conduct the interview and submit a recommendation to the court. Once the defendant is released to the program, the defendant waives his or her right to a speedy trial which likely extends the life of the case.[15] Furthermore, the defendants turned clients of pretrial release programs are subjected to additional agency requirements, such as getting a job, going to counseling, or taking educational classes. From a legal defense standpoint, these mandates may or may not assist in plea negotiations, but they obligate the client beyond the legal parameters of the case, and their compliance with those terms becomes part of the court record. On par with Feeley's (1979) observation that the process is the punishment in the lower courts, the pretrial costs for defendants in OR programs are relatively high: delays, multiple court dates, a confusing process, and competing obligations to their attorney and the caseworker. Public defenders are also aware that their client might not be recommended for release, which reflects poorly on them and risks the possibility that unfavorable information will come to light that unduly biases the judge's view of the case, such as the caseworkers' finding that the defendant is unwilling to address drug or alcohol problems or a history of violence. Caseworkers were cognizant of their potential to prejudice the case and used vague terms to explain why a defendant was denied release, such as "not program amenable."

Sheriff Deputies and Police Officers

The San Miguel Sheriff's Department employs over 700 deputies and administrative staff.[16] The primary function of the sheriff's department is to operate the county jails as well as supervise inmates released to community corrections programs, such as work furloughs. The sheriff's department also provides law enforcement security to the Hall of Justice, including the criminal courtrooms and judicial chambers, and they transport defendants to court hearings throughout the day as well as transport prisoners to and from jails if their housing status changes.

Nonprofit caseworkers come into frequent contact with sheriff's deputies because they conduct interviews with inmates in the various jail facilities. This is a complex relationship since law enforcement officers are generally less inclined to support programs that release arrestees back into the community, many of whom the deputies have seen cycle in and out of the jails for years. In the daily operations, however, I observed little animosity between caseworkers and correctional staff.

My first day working in the jail, however, Samantha Green, a Second Chance caseworker, warned me: "Stay out of the sheriff's way; they don't like or care that we are there and are wary of civilians in the first place and don't look around, don't watch what they are doing, they are paranoid and suspicious of civilians." I found that the relationships between caseworkers and correctional officers were much more nuanced, and at times, genial. I witnessed deputies lend support to caseworkers by helping them to process paperwork and referring other inmates for possible release. Caseworkers, in turn, facilitated positive interactions with deputies and acted in ways to make their jobs easier, which helped them to achieve their advocacy goals. In all, caseworkers and deputies worked along side each other productively, and at times their efforts were mutually beneficial even though they were ideologically working at cross purposes.

Police officers were less directly involved in OR decisions although they hold tremendous discretion at the point of arrest to issue a citation or place the suspect in custody. The citation mandates that they appear in court at a later date to answer to the criminal charge. Reach caseworkers needed a copy of the police report for both pretrial release and probable cause cases. They claimed police officers withheld incident reports to prevent OR petitions from going up for judicial review. Stacy explained another tactic used by the police: "Police officers will ask a judge to up the bail, especially with defendants they think are big drug dealers. They do that before the bail commissioner even sees the case." In this example, raising the bond amount may serve as a subtle cue to the bail commissioner that the defendant should not be released prior to arraignment and further demonstrates the judicial hierarchy as a political arena.

The police and sheriff departments also instituted targeted crime control policies that impinged upon the ability of felony defendants to successfully petition for a nonfinancial release through the Reach program. During my fieldwork tenure, the local police adopted a new nationwide directive called "Operation Cease Fire," to reduce youth gun violence. If an individual was arrested for an offense related to suspected gang activity, the arresting officer faxed a letter to the Reach office stating his or her opposition to OR release. As required, caseworkers attached the memo to the case which then went to the bail commissioner. The memo read:

> Operation Cease Fire is a multiple law enforcement effort to curtail gang violence in the community. This inmate has been arrested due to his/her involvement in violent gang violence. Due to this involvement,

we not feel that this inmate would be a suitable candidate for OR release.

In listening to office talk, I learned that caseworkers became suspicious of the policing directive since a fair number of the charges were dismissed by the prosecutor's office days after their arrest under the new policy. Law enforcement officials also indirectly impacted pretrial release practices during what are informally known as "sweeps." On a periodic basis, multiple social control agencies take into custody fugitives from the law, such as individuals with outstanding warrants and probation violations, which can result in several days of mass arrests and crowded jails. Anthony Banks, a Reach caseworker, said of sweeps: "You can tell by looking at the waiting-to-be-searched tank and the overflow tanks." Staffers cynically claimed it was a politically motivated stratagem to clean up the city. One afternoon, Manuela asserted the jail was busy because "they must be arresting every homeless person in the city" because of President Clinton's impending arrival. Caseworkers rumored when sweeps would take place and alerted their clients to stay off the streets. In a note of irony, the criminal justice system depends on these programs and their staff to help process and release many of the same people back out into the community. In total, this external policing strategy impacted jail operations as well as the ebb and flow staffers' caseloads.

Getting Out: Charting ROR Options at San Miguel

In Goldkamp's (1979) study of bail practices in Philadelphia, there were three decisions that determined release outcomes: granting ROR, denying bail, and setting a bail bond amount. In the San Miguel Courthouse, there are basically three ways to get out of jail prior to arraignment: citation, bail, or own recognizance (OR). The charge dictates whether the defendant is eligible for citation release (promise to appear without judicial approval) or pretrial release (promise to appear with judicial approval) or bail (promise to appear by posting collateral). Most nonviolent misdemeanor offenses are eligible for citation release, but persons arrested for serious misdemeanors, bench warrants,[17] or felony offenses must post bail or be released on their own recognizance. If the arrestee cannot afford to raise bail or he or she does not qualify for citation release, and may come into contact with pretrial release programs. As we will see in the forthcoming chapters, own recognizance decisions are not the same as release outcomes (Demuth 2003). Caseworkers may recommend releases, for example, but the judge rejects the recommendation or the sheriff acquires new information that renders the person ineligible for release, such as probation hold or outstanding warrants in other counties. Conversely, caseworkers can refuse to accept referrals but the judge can invoke his or her authority and mandate that the program take them. This was less common; as we will read in chapter five court officials used more personable methods to cajole program staffers to take on otherwise ineligible offenders.

The criminal justice process begins in earnest once the arrestee is delivered to the county jail and officially booked by the sheriff's deputies into the system. Once at the processing center, individuals are strip-searched, photographed, fingerprinted; they must surrender all markers of their personal identity and connections to the outside social world, such as jewelry and wallets (Goffman 1961). Arrestees step out of their civilian clothing and don bright orange suits to demarcate their inmate status. Custodial mechanisms are in place for surveying and classifying defendants. Inmates are housed in holding tanks, which are grouped according to sex and the various stages of indoctrination, such as the "Awaiting Interview" tank, the "Need Fingerprints" tank, and the "Overflow" tank that is used when the jail is experiencing a surge in the inmate population. Persons classified as exhibiting violent criminal tendencies are segregated from those who are labeled as posing little or no threat. Defendants are also classified according to public health risks: if the inmate is afflicted with HIV, tuberculosis, or hepatitis C (common among incarcerated populations) he or she is classified under the umbrella term of "universal precautions." Inmates assessed to be mentally ill or suicidal are classified under the category of "needs psych [psychiatric] housing" and placed in single occupancy safety cells. The inmate's personal statistics (i.e. race and age) and criminal justice information (i.e. criminal charge) are summarized on a booking card: blue cards indicate the inmate was arrested on a felony offense and white cards are issued to those arrested on misdemeanor offenses. On the front side of the booking card is the inmate's photograph, court number, police report number, and other markers of classification. A jail-booking card is a four by six card with the defendant's name, date of birth, photo, list of criminal charges, and other criminal holds that are keeping the person in custody (e.g. INS or CDC).[18] The back of the card has a row of boxes that tracks the various stages of processing (e.g. medical screening, fingerprinting). The inmate's OR eligibility is one of the boxes that must be checked. As the defendant passes through the various induction stations, the boxes are checked off. Once all the boxes are checked, the newly processed "inmate" is ready to be moved upstairs to the housing facilities.

Reach and Second Chance caseworkers conduct their business in the jail's processing center. Caseworkers first assess if the inmate meets the minimum requirements for release and then conduct a face-to-face interview in their respective offices housed near the sheriff's workstation. The sheriff's deputies permit Reach and Second Chance employees to traffic inmates in and out of their cells to do interviews, a practice called "pulling inmates." Once the caseworker arrives at the jail's processing center, they check out the master key that opens up the holding tanks. Caseworkers identify possible referrals by screening all the new jail booking cards. The booking card box is kept at the deputies' central post and caseworkers check the box at numerous points throughout the day for new arrivals. They then seek approval for the release from the bail commissioner. Aside from these basic similarities, the programs draw on different resources and criteria to assess which inmates become clients.

All persons arrested on felony offenses are processed by the Reach program even if the person is not entitled to ROR due to the nature of the charge. If the person is arrested on an ineligible charge (i.e. drug possession with intent to sell), the case is labeled "Hold for Court." Reach caseworkers prepare the same paperwork as an OR petition but the case is placed directly in court and the judge, not the bail commissioner, will make a release decision at the arraignment hearing. If the bail commissioner grants ROR to the petitioner, caseworkers on the swing shift prepare the necessary forms and return to the jail to inform the inmate that he or she will be released some time that evening. If a defendant is approved for release, he or she is typically out of jail in less than twenty-four hours and ordered to report to Reach for community supervision. The caseworker instructs the client of any conditions placed on his or her release by the court, such as stay away orders from a personal residence, street corner, or commercial establishment. The caseworker processes the release paperwork with the county clerk's office for certification which is then filed with the sheriff's department. Staff affirmed and I observed that it takes twenty-four to forty-eight hours to process an OR case. If the bail commissioner denies pretrial release, the arrestee is detained pending arraignment or posting bail. If detained at arraignment, the judge may consider granting them unsupervised OR release (they do not have to report to a pretrial release worker). If the judge denied a nonfinancial release option, the defense attorney may make a motion to reduce bail. Bail commissioners and judges reported to me that they often denied release through the Reach program because they wanted the defendant to be considered for participation in the Open Door program for more intensive supervision.

Defendants arrested on misdemeanor warrants will likely come into contact with the Second Chance caseworkers. It is important to note that these defendants are facing two criminal charges. The first offense is the underlying misdemeanor charge (i.e. petty theft) for which they were mandated to answer to in court and the second offense is failing to appear to court (i.e. the bench warrant). Defendants must meet the county sheriff's basic eligibility criteria in order to be referred to the program, which includes persons originally charged with burglary, drug possession, prostitution, vandalism, or driving with a suspended license. Defendants are ineligible if they are arrested or charged for any felonies, domestic violence, weapons possession, or failure to appear for a jury trial.

If they meet the basic criteria, the caseworker makes a copy of the booking card, types their name into the court management system to access their court appearance record and criminal justice history. Staff closely reviews these documents to get a sense of the person's court compliance history and to look for any previous arrests for assault or weapons. It is important to note that a defendant with a criminal record of arrests or convictions for violent, threatening, or assaultive behavior does not necessarily preclude the caseworker from recommending the case in chambers. If the bail commissioner grants the release petition, the arrestee is released within a few hours and mandated to return to court the following morning. In court, the majority of the charges are eventually dismissed or reduced to a lesser offense (i.e. infractions). If the petitioner is not eligible or denied release, they spend the night in jail and go to court the next morning. I estimate that releases were quickly processed by the staff within a few hours.

Open Door and Pathways caseworkers most often come into contact with new referrals after the defendant is processed, criminally charged, and moved upstairs to await the next phase of the criminal court process. Caseworkers held many interviews in the jail's housing pods, at the communal tables, or in empty dayrooms. On less frequent occasions, caseworkers conducted interviews in several small rooms near the sheriff's portal in the old section of the jail. Judges and public defenders typically referred defendants to Open Door and Pathways directly from court at the early stages of adjudication, typically the arraignment or the preliminary hearing. After the interview, caseworkers submitted positive or negative recommendations for release, usually within two to three days. If they are accepted by the program, the judge signs the necessary forms which are also filed for certification with the clerk's office and sheriff's department. By the day's end, the defendant is brought back down to the processing center, picked up by an Open Door caseworker, and escorted to the office for program orientation. Pathways may also pick up the defendant from jail or direct them to come to the office the next day to design a treatment plan. If the defendant is rejected by the program, they remain in jail with the possibility of a bail reduction or ROR. If the prosecutor reduces charges, the judge or public defender may re-refer the defendant for pretrial release services.

Conclusion

In summary, the bail reform movement, jail overcrowding crisis, and emergence of pretrial release programs represent a significant shift in the institutional supports and discretionary powers that determine who gets out of the San Miguel county jail. The chapter also mapped out the new criminal justice terrain and how the various courthouse stakeholders influence pretrial release practices. The empirical sections will explore the various ways in which the interagency arrangements positively and adversely impact release decisions and outcomes as well as the possibilities for informal diversion. In the next chapter, I focus on the construct of caseworkers as professionals without papers to reflect their complex role in the courthouse community. I examine in greater detail the constraints, contingencies, and competing values that impinge upon caseworkers' ability to live up to their idealized roles as alternative justice specialists. Specifically, I claim that caseworkers walk a fine line between advocacy and accountability, rights and privileges, and authority and power.

---

[1] Defendants who appear in court in civilian clothes (as opposed to inmate garb), for example, have been shown to have favorable case outcomes.

[2] In Flemming's (1982) study of felony bail decisions, he found that release before trial can positively impact criminal case outcomes for defendants.

[3] The early bail reform movement efforts successfully established a variety of pretrial release options (involving either non-financial provisions or release through a small percentage of the set bail) for misdemeanor and felony defendants.

[4] The legislation also sought to equal bail practices by setting new bail guidelines.

[5] Of the 171 programs that participated in the review, fifteen percent have started since 2000. One half of the programs started since 1990 are administratively housed in the county probation department. The increase in probation-run programs is due in part to the growth of pretrial release services in rural areas. Data suggest that these smaller jurisdictions merge services in an effort to best utilize limited resources.

[6] Staff members reported that they made conservative choices in large part because of the small staff and mixed sentiments from police officers who

imposed restrictions on obtaining the necessary documentation to present the case to a judge such as the person's criminal history.

[7] A bail bondsmen group was successful in shutting down a pretrial release program in Broward County, Florida. http://www.scpr.org/news/2010/01/22 /bondsman-lobby-targets-pretrial-release-programs/ (Accessed on October 22nd 2010).

[8] During the first year of operation, grant monies from a local foundation funded the program services. In 1997, the program secured monies from the Mayor's Criminal Justice Office and pretrial release services were then formally contracted through the Sheriff's Department.

[9] The Reach program was composed of six men and ten women. The agency was staffed by persons of diverse racial and ethnic backgrounds including persons of African American, Caucasian, Asian American, and Hispanic descent.

[10] The demographic characteristics of the Second Chance staff included two men and three women. Of the five employees, two persons were Hispanic and three were Caucasian.

[11] Pathways was staffed by two women and two men. Of the four employees, all were Caucasian. I did one interview one former employee who was African American.

[12] Open Door employed two women and seven men. Like Reach, the organizational makeup of the nonprofit was diverse including persons of African American, Asian American, and Hispanic descent.

[13] The municipal courts handled misdemeanors and crimes with bail under 25,000 and superior courts handled felonies. The municipal court judges were the first to see all arrestees because they were processed pretrial releases and bail decisions. In effect, these meant that misdemeanor judges were making decisions about felonies cases. A misdemeanor judge would finish the calendar by two in the afternoon. Superior court judges, comparatively, were running trials until four in the afternoon and then managing settlement conferences afterwards.

[14] Bail Commissioner Delaney was elected to judge during my fieldwork.

[15] This datum was obtained during several interviews with pretrial release caseworkers.

[16] The department has been led by Sheriff Donna Michaels for a number of years. During her tenure she has demonstrated a strong commitment to jail alternative programs and cost effective and humane detention facilities.

[17] Typically, judges issue bench warrants for persons who fail to appear for a mandated court appearance on a pending criminal charge. When a law enforcement officer arrests an individual who has a bench warrant, he or she is incarcerated in the county jail and a new court date is scheduled. Persons arrested on bench warrants are commonly considered flight risks, meaning there is a high likelihood that they will not appear for their court date if released.

[18] Immigration and Naturalization Services (INS) and California Department of Corrections (CDC).

3
Nonprofit Casework in Context

Each year around Christmas time, the Open Door invites judges, attorneys, court staffers, and community group leaders to the agency for food and festivities in celebration of another successful year working together. This annual event was particularly significant because it marked the opening of their new facility, The Community Treatment Center, that offered counseling, life skills, and employment services to court-referred defendants. Open Door Director Wayne Brooks prefaced his remarks to the staff with a baseball analogy to set the tone for his speech. He told of how during the World Series the manager of the local team knew they were all on the verge of something great; he didn't know what would happen but he was savoring the moment. "People are watching us very closely now to see what we do and eighty percent of those people are hoping that we fail," in the same way, "because our success is a threat to them."

He mocked bureaucracies, saying "nothing is achieved." Open Door's goal, by contrast, is to "intervene in court and cut down on bureaucracy." The director reminded the staff that at a time when the city and state are in debt and cutting costs, the agency is facing a growth opportunity. "The best time for change is crisis," he added. This holiday season was the first time in twenty years that the organization's revenue had gone up. The agency's caseload was likely to increase because the sheriff's department had to cut ten million dollars from its budget and wanted to know if pretrial release program could expand its services. The program director closed his remarks by saying: "We are moving values from one place to another, to change the way things are done. [We are] one step beyond intake and assessment; now the goal for clients is intake, assessment, immediacy, and accessibility. Remember when we couldn't spell 'assessment'?"

***

The pretrial release caseworkers in this study frequently described their everyday tasks by saying, "It's not just any job." Indeed, it is not. Nonprofits as agents of the state are increasingly influential in the administration of law yet we know little about the tools and decision making practices that community-based organizations utilize to effect criminal justice policy making (Roman et al 2002). Outside agencies are contracted to evaluate offenders' eligibility and suitability for OR release and then pass on risk factors to court officials in order to make lawful decisions. Nonprofit caseworkers are more than information gatherers; they are key participants in the courthouse community, and they import humanitarian ideals about how to respond to criminal behavior. As evident in the above vignette, nonprofits are also organizational actors vying for territorial expansion, economic growth, and occupational advancements. How do nonprofits carry out their social justice agenda in the cultural milieu of contractual governance? Researchers and practitioners surmise that partnerships between nonprofits and governmental agencies are mutually beneficial and allow for greater flexibility to determine the methods and levels of public service (Brinkerhoff 2002; Coston 1998; DeHoog 1990; Salamon 1987; Young 2000) which reflects certain assumptions about participants' common goals, shared liability, and equal decision making powers. How do these partnerships operate in practice? Do nonprofits in joint ventures with state entities surrender aspects of their ideological beliefs and organizational priorities? One of the central debates in the public policy literature is whether nonprofits lose their autonomy due to governmental coerciveness and demands for accountability. Conversely, what are the implications for public services for the polity when they are administered by outsourced agents? I consider how nonprofits afoot in the criminal justice system concurrently advanced their advocacy agenda and legitimated their reputational status as professional agents of the court. I draw primarily on nonprofit staffers' own accounts and my observations of their occupational experiences, which culminates into a narrative of how they perceive of their roles and responsibilities in relationship to defendants and court officials.

The Fine Lines

The coming sections, *Keying the Iron Cage*, *Objectifying Values*, and *Qualifying Expertise* explore how caseworkers walked a fine line between their commitment to reforming systemic injustices and conforming to the expectations of a government sponsor. In Keying the Iron Cage outside providers broadened the eligibility parameters to increase the number of defendants released on their own recognizance, but their definitions of legal entitlement also labeled some petitioners as bad risks for pretrial services. Objectifying Values illustrates that nonprofits' restorative justice aims were increasingly compromised by subsuming bureaucratically oriented tasks and institutional pressures to quantify their efficaciousness in reducing recidivism. In Qualifying Expertise caseworkers played up their skills to augment their professional standing and played down their influential power to negotiate status differences. These fine lines reveal the underlying conflicts and collaborations that comprise the politics of contractual governance. This chapter also serves as a foregrounding for the empirical analyses on how caseworkers screened defendants as potential clients, negotiated pretrial release parameters with law trained actors, orchestrated courtroom theater to move cases towards adjudication, and policed defendants' compliance with the conditions of their release.

Keying the Iron Cage

The primary activity of jail alternative programs was evaluating whether a defendant could be safely released into the community pending the disposition of the criminal matter. Many defendants had little in the way of resources to post bond and they lacked an understanding of criminal procedures. Consequently, they often failed to represent themselves well before a magistrate, pled to bad deals, and missed court dates. Without financial resources and traditional forms of legal capital, defendants looked to pretrial release programs as their best chance to get out of jail and resume productive lives. Caseworkers' interviewing instruments and oral representations of legal cases directly benefited defendants who might otherwise remain in custody pending adjudication of their criminal cases.

On a fundamental level, nonprofits were empowered to get people out of jail by virtue of the fact that they were allowed access to sites of institutional control. Caseworkers were in possession of the keys to the back corridors of the courthouse and they filed through this restricted entry to meet with judges and attorneys in chambers to discuss legal problems. They were authorized to open cell doors in the jail's processing center and escort inmates to their offices to conduct interviews soon after their arrest. Caseworkers also made an effort to "walk the line" as they so called it by answering questions from inmates about the status of their criminal cases and actively looking for unlawful detainments. By granting nonprofits the "keys to the iron cage," these outside providers, in the interest of their advocacy roles, widened the net of possible releases. As we will read, they aided defendants by strengthening otherwise weak pretrial petitions, brokering pleas for judicial leniency, and mediating the court's attempt to punish noncompliance. This is exemplified by Wayne's statement during a staff meeting, "Our goals are to increase the number of referrals and releases, increase dismissals, and decrease sentences." "We really try to let out everyone we can," echoed Mindy Demarco, a Second Chance supervisor.

In Flemming's book, *Punishment before Trial*, he argues that the substantive factors that stipulate pretrial release decisions are uncertainty (lack of accurate and complete information), risk (person's threat to public safety), and resources (staffing and available jail beds) (1982). The notion of Keying the Iron Cage unpacks how caseworkers formulated risk categories to get defendants out of jail and resolved criminal matters in non-punitive ways as well as kept defendants in jail by rejecting referrals or terminating clients from the caseload.[1] To make release decisions, caseworkers employed locally informed criteria to evaluate individuals for pretrial services. What does risk and risk assessment mean when the decision is outsourced to nonprofits? During my field studies, I began to theorize that the worth of a case was informed by both statute definitions of criminality as well as culturally prescribed values of personal responsibility, honesty, and redemption. Caseworkers drew on a set of interpretative tools to rationalize court referrals into three general classifications: duds (bad risks), clients (good risks) and wobblers (wavering between good and bad risks). This is similar to what Loseke (2003) calls "social problems formula stories" (140) in that these risk categories acted as organizational benchmarks for assessing whether the defendant could be managed in the contexts of the agency's resources and behavioral expectations. The screening process was premised on two sets of criteria: eligibility and suitability. Eligibility criteria were objectively determined by the defendant's criminal charge, legal history, and in some cases the criminal status (e.g. parole and probation). Suitability criteria, however, were much more subjective because decisions were influenced by staffers' moral compasses not procedural law. Caseworkers listened to defendants' stories and assessed their program amenability according to certain types of troubles. For example, defendants with more sympathetic stories, such as the homeless, were evaluated differently than persons judged to be lazy and dangerous. Reach staffer Anthony Banks for example described the type of people he believed should be released. He said, "The people that have regular lives and got into a fight, and might miss their construction job on Monday...we don't want those people laid off

[work]. We want to restore status quo." As an important consequence, some defendants were labeled as more entitled to release than others.

While pretrial release staffers identified themselves as social justice advocates for poor defendants, the demands of their jobs on the front lines echoed conventional approaches to rationing public services in a manner reminiscent of street level workers (Lipsky 1980; Smith and Lipsky 1993). Caseworkers wanted to keep caseload numbers manageable, assist motivated clients, and maintain a low failure to appear (FTA) rate. They employed on the spot discretion to evaluate individual troubles in the face of limited time and information, large caseloads, pushy public defenders, and obdurate prosecutors. The dilemma of all street level bureaucrats is how to reconcile the bureaucratic rules with the complex social problems presented by clientele. Tracy King, an Open Door caseworker, remarked, "I don't have time to mess with clients that don't do anything." Nonprofit staffers developed programmatic criteria to screen out defendants by drawing on their past personal experiences with clientele and taking into consideration limited organizational resources to meet the demands of growing caseloads, what Open Door caseworkers called "tough love" and Pathways caseworkers called "being realistic." Pathways caseworkers typically did not accept defendants with serious mental illnesses or who did not show motivation to get off the streets. Pathways Staffer Paul Lewis explained, "There are very few clients that make our job really easy. Most clients make our job difficult in some way." At a moment's notice, caseworkers had to stopgap the unpredictable crises in clients' lives, such as getting kicked out of the shelter or residential hotel, showing up to the office drunk or high, not taking their psychiatric medication, becoming depressed, and refusing to make progress on the treatment plan. Staffers took into account how a potential client would impact their workload if released to the community. Paul said of his previous job working with troubled juveniles: "Kids deserve many chances to turn their lives around but I don't feel that way about adults so much." Likewise, Second Chance staffers did not present cases to the bail commissioner if the defendant did not have a good reason for missing his or her court date.

In total, these referral practices suggest that caseworkers evaluated defendants with a view towards maintaining their own standards of a good risk while, at the same time, challenging or expanding judges' parameters of a good referral. In contemplation of the forthcoming empirical chapters, I suggest that outsourcing judicial decision making powers to nonprofits blurred the lines between rights and privileges in terms of who was granted pretrial release. The nonprofits in this study operated in an increasingly competitive environment, and, as we will read, they modified their goals and retooled their resources and technologies to bring their agencies into alignment with political shifts in the courthouse community to which I now turn to in the next section.

Objectifying Values

In Kleinman's (1996) study of Renewal, members were drawn to the alternative health organization by a deeply-held belief in doing something meaningful, something good with their lives, what the author calls a "moral identity" (5). The staff eschewed middle class conformity and its materialist trappings to collectively do more with less for the betterment of society. Similarly, a common denominator among the pretrial release caseworkers was an aspiration to make a qualitative difference in the lives of defendants, their families, and their communities, what I call an alternative justice identity. Caseworkers often said that they loved their jobs because they can "make a difference." They wanted their work to positively impact the structural inequality of the justice system that disproportionately affected poor and underrepresented groups. This was evident because staff persons were involved with other types of human rights work and actively campaigned to improve the socioeconomic conditions for immigrant groups, build affordable housing for poor families, and mentor disadvantaged youth. "I think the word for it is advocacy. Our greater work is systemic change because it shows that restorative justice can work," explained Caseworker Mario Alvarez during an interview at the Open Door. In many ways their work in jails and courtrooms was part of a larger occupational calling. On my first day shadowing Dave Powell, a Pathways caseworker, he said standing on the steps outside the Hall of Justice: "I went to law school. I dropped out. God wanted me to be here (pointing at the courthouse) in a different form: to help people." During the day shift working in the jail's processing center, Staffer Natasha Lee explained how she came to her job at Reach. She said, "I wanted a job working in jail [and] helping defendants. I did prison work in college, working on prison issues." Second Chance worker Taj Ramirez explained during an interview, "There is a sense that this is a necessary job. I don't believe we should be criminalizing the poor, criminalizing women, so that is a little minor stand." And so, for nonprofit staffers the job of providing free pretrial release services to people who could not afford bail represented an extension of how they saw themselves ideologically.

Outsourcing judicial decision making to private nonprofits however complicates the conventional role expectations in the courthouse community. From both a theoretical and practical standpoint, caseworkers practice their trade in the courtroom with an orientation that is different from law-trained actors (Lidz and Walker 1977; Munetz and Teller 2003; Whiteacre 2007). Traditional court functionaries rely upon coercive measures to ensure the offender conforms to court mandates and levy sanctions in response to criminal acts for purposes of punishment as well as deterrence. Caseworkers, by comparison, seek to treat individuals internally by helping them to adopt productive and healthy behaviors (Lidz and Walker 1977; Margolin 1997). The jail alternative principles proffered by nonlegal caseworkers came into conflict with the correctional mindset of law enforcement officials. The opposing ambitions (Kleinman 1996) between traditional and alternative approaches to crime-related problems are expressed by Samantha Green, a Second Chance caseworker: "[The criminal justice system] has a different set of agendas, different feelings on punishment and what is criminal [than we do]" Victor Smith of the Open Door said to me: "We don't want to be like probation. We are more proactive. We do transports and call agencies. I've rarely seen a probation officer give a report in court."

In objectifying values, nonprofits mediated the interstices between their alternative justice aims and increasing pressures to professionalize their operations. Caseworkers under government contract faced both internal and external demands to make transparent the ways in which their decision making practices reduced costs, protected public safety, and positively reintegrated offenders back into their community, what Crawford (2003) calls "active responsibility." Up until 2002, the nonprofit programs were funded by the county through noncompetitive multiyear contracts. During the time of my study, the sheriff's department required that each nonprofit competitively bid to contract for pretrial release services in the face of tightening budgets for jail services. Director Lawrence Austin of Second Chance explained, "The sheriff's department can no longer afford to have these same kinds of relationships [with nonprofits]; they need to be as cost effective as possible now." The value of caseworkers' job performances was then increasingly measured by the percentage of release recommendations to denials and the number of accepted clients in compliance with the court. To demonstrate their efficacy, the agencies instituted new procedures to make better and faster release decisions. Supervisor Lee Mitchell said to me during an informal conversation at the agency: "[The Open Door] had to become much more proactive. We couldn't just sit back on our cases and turn in papers." The agencies purchased or upgraded advanced technologies to better manage client information. Open Door supervisors often carried a laptop computer into the courtroom to access client files, provide up to date information on cases to court officials quickly, and immediately process new referrals. A computer database is similar to a dossier (Foucault 1979) in that it is a comprehensive source of information that tracked release decisions, the defendant's treatment history, and the status of the legal case in court. The use of technological resources also granted nonprofits a measure of legitimacy in the courtroom setting. Wayne said:

> People don't realize that we are a business. [People] still think we're a nonprofit organization, a laid back place. No, we're becoming institutionalized and we have to do things differently now. This is a profession. [We are] evolving but outsiders don't see that we are still learning.

The managerial push to quantify the nonprofit's fiscal and systemic impact, however, undermined caseworkers' efforts to prioritize client advocacy. Some of the nonprofits' tier of middle managers accused their subordinates of fewer releases because they were perceived as being less committed to social justice causes. Open Door Supervisor John Parks opined: "I miss the radical staff of the old guard. They had awareness in their communities, of being out there, like the networking and grassroots stuff. The staff is no longer like that. They are too caught up in the database and the paperwork. The new guard has broken down the old guard." John suggests that current organizational practices resulted in caseworkers' protecting their liability for pretrial release decisions which negatively impacted the sheer number of releases. Ironically the database adversely affected the organizational goal of increasing caseloads because it required that staffers concretize their release recommendations by accumulating more paperwork. Indeed, Tracy affirmed:

> We [used to] take everybody because all you had to do was fill out [one] screen. Gradually we had to fill out more and more screens. We started to take less people because it meant so much work; we started looking for ways to deny people.

The database also made vulnerable aspects of caseworkers' jobs to managerial scrutiny. Staffers protected their job performance rates by more selectively screening referrals. At the Open Door, Mario often had the highest (failed to appear) FTA rate. He had sixty-eight clients on his caseload and said to me that he was concerned because "Three of my clients failed to appear in court last week. I worry about my failure to appear rate." After a quarterly meeting with Wayne to discuss their job performance, Lee, (Caseworker) Steve Brown, Mario, and Tracy returned to their cubicles. Their moods were somber; the meeting had not gone well. Tracy, who had the highest percentage of denials, was clearly frustrated. She said, "I'll have a caseload of 100 but then I'll have a high FTA rate like Mario. So, which is it? More releases or low FTA rates?"

Nonprofit staffers with social justice ideals perceived that working in the institutional confines of the justice system compromised their occupational aspirations. Vince pondered aloud his initial reluctance to take the job as we walked from the office to the jail across the street. He said, "I was just out of college and I needed a job. I was interested in more community organizing, direct action type work. I wasn't sure I wanted to be this institutional. I found a lot of limitations in terms of what kind of casework I wanted to do." Vince's statement points to a larger concern among caseworkers that their jobs would be co-opted as a bureaucratic arm of the court. This occurred when the Reach board of directors no longer permitted staffers to recommend releases which adversely affected Supervisor Stacy Abaya's sense of her job importance. She said, "Before we were a big part of people getting released. [Now] It doesn't seem like we have much of a caseload...that's one of the hardest things." In another example, Steve lamented that the agency's push to modernize casework undermined client advocacy since the database cannot quantify the more meaningful aspects of his work. He said:

> Why can't we measure the program's success by how many people got more stable housing, got in substance abuse treatment, and went to counseling? There is really no way to measure those things. Some clients don't finish the program but they come back and tell us that the program changed their lives for the better.

Nonprofit agencies put their reputations on display by generating monthly, quarterly, and annual reports on the high percentages of defendants who complied with the terms of their release. These crisp one-page reports are a powerful demonstration of caseworkers' fiscal impact on the jail bed numbers. Nonprofit agencies built their pretrial release reputations by framing criminal justice problems in ways that resonated with traditional justice actors. Taj explained that the organizational value of the Second Chance program was tied to how much money it saved the sheriff's department. He said:

> This is a nonprofit, so we truly believe that we can do better than putting people in jail. The challenge for Second Chance is how to negotiate the politics of the [criminal justice] system. The sheriff's office is in the business of putting people in jail but we want to get them out. There is a big contradiction. They have the power and the money and we don't. How do you keep pushing an [advocacy] agenda when everyone wants to put people in jail? Second Chance has been able to make a good case because we save [the jail] money. We save them $100 a day per jail bed, that's how you have to frame it, when in reality we don't care about the money. We actually want to get people out because it is wrong to incarcerate poor people, but no one will give [us] money for that.

Taj's statement is similar to how Renewal members espoused the ideals of equality and democracy, yet they felt compelled to embrace conventional ways of organizing to bring greater recognition and legitimacy to their cause, such as using Robert's Rules of Order which unwittingly bureaucratized the structure of board meetings (Kleinman 1996). In a similar way, nonprofits generated fiscal reports to advertise that jail alternative programs were effective. These organizational technologies acted as "authority props" (Kleinman 1996: 37) meaning that they symbolized the organization's efforts to gain external legitimacy. The Second Chance, Pathways, Open Door, and Reach programs sought to make accountable their routine work practices to gain recognition as accredited entities in the criminal courts.

The nonprofits also objectified their values by undertaking additional criminal justice responsibilities that ultimately conflicted with its substantive mission. The presiding judge asked Reach to take on the task of compiling probable cause cases in addition to pretrial release cases for judicial review. In 1991, the Supreme Court ruled that all defendants in custody must have their arrests reviewed by a judicial officer to ensure that the police had just cause to make the arrest.[2] Probable cause must be determined within forty-eight hours of the arrest. Failure to establish "just cause" may result in dismissal of the defendant's criminal charge and immediate release from custody. Reach director, Carol Whitney, noted that the nonprofit's role as an information gatherer constituted the agency as "a natural fit" for the task. Stacy explained that Reach took on the responsibility in hopes it would wed the agency closer to the criminal justice system. She said, "Probable cause gives us power with the courts because they need us to do [it] in forty-eight hours. If we didn't have that power, than what good are we? We need it to have negotiating power in the future." Echoing a similar sentiment, Anthony Banks, a caseworker, said, "[Probable cause] cements us into the criminal justice system." However, the practice came under scrutiny on the grounds that it was a judicial function not a pretrial release function. Members of nonprofit's board of directors argued that the task represented an ideological dilemma because the process helped to ensure defendants stayed in jail, while Reach should help defendants get released from jail. Anthony explained, "Without probable cause, we could do a lot more; we could interview more people, there wouldn't be a time limit." At times, I observed Carol directing caseworkers to prioritize probable cause cases over pretrial release cases when the agency was short staffed. To return to their social justice roots would required that the nonprofit yield established occupational territory which, in turn, potentially risked their future bargaining power as a contracted entity. The push and pull of objectifying values revealed that for caseworkers to realize their alternative visions of justice, certain things may be compromised along the way. They experienced institutional pressures to demonstrate their competencies as agents of the court because they are increasingly dependent upon government contracts to survive.

Qualifying Expertise

We know little about the occupational characteristics of nonprofit caseworkers in terms of what training, education, experiences, or expertise they bring to their position in the judicial system. Demographically, the makeup of this sample is similar to the Pretrial Justice Institute (2009) survey which reported that one third of pretrial release personnel held bachelor's degrees as their highest education attainment and fifty-two percent of persons were aged twenty-six to forty-five. The estimated median age for the nonprofit caseworkers in my study was twenty-eight.[3] Qualifying expertise considers how caseworkers developed a work identity as "professionals without papers." By this I mean that agency employees have influential powers to shape the legal consequences for criminal defendants yet the majority of staff do not have licenses, educational credentials, or specialized training specific to their tasks as criminal justice workers. This fact did not go unnoticed by traditional court functionaries. Caseworkers' increasing presence in legal decision making venues raised suspicion and curiosity among court officials. When the Open Door first started to provide pretrial services, Wayne recalled during our interview: "We were met with real resistance from the probation department. [We] were called paraprofessionals; probation said we couldn't do [the work]." The term paraprofessional is a job title given to persons in various occupations, including education, accounting, healthcare, and law who are trained to assist practiced professionals but are not themselves certified in that particular line of work. Lee suggested that caseworkers' quasi-legal courthouse roles placed them in a precarious position because they had no formal legal standing. While we waited for a felony preliminary hearing to commence, he said to me:

> We walk a fine line. We don't have any professional credentials yet we have all this influence in court. Sometimes the district attorney and public defender say, 'who are these people?'

This is similar to Halliday and his colleagues who observed that social workers in Scottish courts held a "relative professional status" (2009: 407) in that they felt a sense of uncertainty working in the legal domain and they sought to augment their position in the courts by professionalizing their activities. To augment their status as "professionals without papers" they qualified their expertise by showcasing their discretionary powers to manage defendant populations. During an interview with Stacy, she implied that caseworkers were better able to assess risk. She said, "We're the only ones actually talking to the person and the judge just sees paper." They asserted a degree of informational authority by nature of their ability to read and understand archaic crime-related printouts and assumed technical tasks to leverage their position in the judicial system. Stacy explained: "We're the only agency that runs raps with Local, State, Federal, and DMV. You have to go through a program to learn how to read [the reports]." Many bail commissioners and judges have difficulty reading rap sheets and have come to rely on caseworkers' summations to make release decisions. Caseworker Rueben Keifer noted, "In my opinion, summarizing the rap sheet is the most important work that we've done that really anchored [Reach]." Indeed, Reach has the right to use criminal justice information that ordinarily only law enforcement agencies can access.

Caseworkers' recognized competence for getting things done was apparent given the fact that judges made different decisions because they followed caseworkers' counsel. Victor said in regards to the nonprofits' unique contribution to criminal court processing:

> We are doing something nobody else is doing. No one else is doing the kind of CM we are doing. No one is taking a client directly out of jail

and placing them directly into a program. I look at that as being awesome. Eventually, I think it's going to become national. I think it's a good thing.

While caseworkers actively played up their skills and expertise, they expressed concern about causing undue influence and transgressing role boundaries. In my interview with Natasha, she explained: "It's taboo" to ask commissioners about their release decisions. She continued, "It's tricky territory and there's this respect thing where you can't get too friendly with the judges. To ask them, 'why didn't you [release] this guy?' is bordering on [that] territory.'" Similarly, Kelsey Martinez of the Open Door articulated the need to maintain a delicate equilibrium. She said, "We are definitely there to advocate for the client but we are neutral in terms of how we relate to the court actors." Caseworkers recognized that their lack of credentialed expertise placed limits on the nature and scope of their formal role. For example, Dave said: "We have to be careful what we say to clients. We can't give legal advice and we can't tell the client what's going to happen next. We have no power in that respect." Given caseworkers' extensive access to and communication with courtroom judges, they worried about disclosing too much information and biasing the judge's view of the case. Lee explained to me, "Judges operate in a vacuum. It is deliberate because they need to remain as objective as possible" in relationship to a pending criminal matter. Staffers then softened the appearance of being influential out of concern that they would be perceived as overstepping the boundaries of their prescribed roles as well as in the interest of preserving the merits of procedural law.

Comparatively, staffers, in deference to sheriffs' deputies, feigned ignorance of certain procedures to acquire additional knowledge and to advance their advocacy goals. Second Chance caseworkers helped the sheriff's deputies to process the district attorney's rebooking sheets in search of referrals that would otherwise fall through the cracks due to bureaucratic mistakes or oversights.[4] Caseworkers looked for additional releases under the guise of helping deputies to process the paperwork. Mindy explained:

We don't frame it like 'we are looking for your errors.' The way we present [the problem] is non-threatening. When you are dealing with people in positions of power, you have to [guard] their ego.

Caseworkers also downplayed their influence over the release decision to limit their liability for denials. I often heard Reach caseworkers say to defendants at the end of the interview, "It's up to the judge" and Second Chance caseworkers said to me that they would tell defendants that "The judge denied you" if they opted not to present the case at all. Taj explained, "It's easier on them and easier on us." He continued:

> What I have learned to do the hard way is to be very clear and direct with instructions. This way they understand that it is not up to me to make the decision; it is up to the judge. It is not an automatic release and there is a chance they might stay over. So, when I say [to the defendant] 'look you're not going to get out, your rap is too hard core, or the reference didn't come thorough' so they know what the deal is. Before I developed my own style, I would not be clear on the decision-making process and then they would go off because they thought it was a done deal. I was accused of misleading them. I got hit a couple of times. So now I make sure they know I am not the one making the decision.

These examples illustrate that caseworkers saw it their advantage to uncouple their actions from the release outcomes by downplaying their influential power. In total, caseworkers orchestrated efforts to play up and play down their authority hints at the precarious nature of power relations when justice is outsourced to private nonprofit organizations.

Conclusion

This chapter explored how caseworkers walked a fine line between client advocacy and government accountability which necessarily impacted pretrial release practices. In doing so, I further explored how outsourcing legal decision making to nonprofits redefined notions of risk, power and justice in the courthouse community. It is important to contextualize nonprofit casework in the broader political and organizational settings. The involvement of nonprofits in pretrial release services demonstrates that efforts to reform criminal justice processes are not limited to ways that make the legal system smaller, better, more accountable, but rather there are also creative ways of making routine justice more accessible to poor and minority groups. Pretrial release caseworkers however faced a unique set of opportunities and challenges in bringing about jail alternatives which directly impacted a defendant's likelihood of getting out of jail.

Caseworkers are also situated in complex ways vis-à-vis the arrestees and court officials as well as the outsourced agencies that they work for. Staffers wanted to be thought of as court professionals and to demonstrate that they are sufficiently capable of supervising criminal offenders. Yet caseworkers' jobs are difficult: they work with a challenging population and, often lacking formal training, must routinely negotiate the complexities of the justice system. Their status as professionals without papers placed some limitations on their actions due to the court's expectations for organizational performance. Caseworkers' strategies for managing these fine lines are dependent upon how well they are orchestrated in tandem with other courthouse actors as well as the internal constraints on and opportunities for exercising their autonomy. In total, nonprofit workers, as agents of the court, had to strike a balance between their building reputations as trustworthy risk assessors and taking more risks to meet their advocacy goals.

As we will read in the forthcoming empirical chapters, nonprofit caseworkers expanded their occupational territory into judging, lawyering, and policing functions which not only resulted in moving cases to different institutional outcomes but also portended moving values between the nonprofit and legal domains. The next chapter brings into view the county jail as a critical site where caseworkers talked to defendants about their legal problems and private troubles. Caseworkers developed interviewing practices for screening potential clients in ways that advantaged and disadvantaged a person's chances of getting released.

---

[1] The concept of *Keying the Iron Cage* draws on two classic sociological ideas to capture how the organizational structure and culture of the lower courts shaped nonprofit caseworkers' capacity to affect incarceration rates. The Iron Cage (Weber 1952) refers to increasing restrictions on individual freedoms in rational bureaucracies. Caseworkers keyed or reframed the way cases were presented to package problems to justify their decision making and persuade others to support their way of looking at the world (Goffman 1974).

[2] Probable cause is an outcome of Riverside v. Mclaughlin (500 U.S. 44 1991).

[3] I did not inquire specifically about age during my interviews.

[4] The district attorney has prosecutorial discretion to pursue, reduce or dismiss the criminal charges levied against the defendant (Albonetti 1986; Davis 2007). The district attorney's decision to prosecute alleged criminal activity is based on sufficient evidence, the defendant's criminal status and a decision as to whether pursuing the case is in the interest of justice. This charging decision is typically made within 48 hours of the arrest and logged on rebooking sheets. After 5pm, the rebooking sheets are delivered the sheriff's department. Deputies examined the rebooking sheets as a mean to manage the jail population. Once the district attorney amended or dropped charges, some inmates were eligible for pretrial release. Consider this example. A person is arrested and jailed on two counts: a new felony offense and a misdemeanor bench warrant for failing

to appear to court on another case.   At rebooking, defendant may become eligible for Second Chance if the district attorney drops the felony charge because the only charge holding them in jail is misdemeanor bench warrant.

4

Screening Potential Clients

On a Friday morning, the jail was very busy and Anthony Banks, a Reach caseworker, had twelve interviews to complete. Carl was the first interview of the day and he was housed in Tank B. Anthony stuck the oversized key into the lock, gripped the door handle, turned the key twice around and pulled hard. The cell door popped open. This action immediately caught the attention of the eight inmates inside. Anthony escorted Carl, a forty-four-year-old Caucasian man, into the small Reach office. Carl's jail card was stamped "Homeless" and his hard life on the streets was visible in his tired eyes, overgrown beard, and blackened fingernails. Carl slumped down in the assigned interviewee seat, placed his elbows on the desk, and buried his head in his hands. Anthony, poised to begin the interview, did not seem taken aback. He grabbed a handful of forms: white for the interview, purple for the rap sheet, and yellow for the form that the bail commissioner would sign if he authorized the release. They sat in silence and then Anthony asked, "Are you ok?" "No, I'm not," said Carl with an undertone of desperation and rage, tears welling up in his eyes. Carl stumbled through an account of how his long time girlfriend had just died and that the "fucking cops" had arrested him last night for a "bogus" charge (drug possession). To make matters worse, the jail was overcrowded, which meant it was taking a long time to process all the new arrestees. Carl pounded on the desk, telling Anthony that he had been in the overflow tank since the previous afternoon. In the overflow tank, there are no beds to sleep in, no hot food to eat (inmates are given bag lunches), and no showers. Anthony tried to conduct the interview by assuring him that Reach was his best bet to get out of jail. Carl was so visibly upset, citing the injustice of his detainment, that Anthony did not even ask him all the necessary questions. Anthony took Carl back to the overflow tank and made a note on the interview sheet that Carl was too distraught to complete the interview. He had eleven more to do. Because Carl's case was incomplete, Anthony did not submit it to the bail commissioner.

This meant that Carl would have to wait to go to court before being considered for release on his own recognizance.

**

The California penal statute provides general provisions and guidelines for making a judicial determination for pretrial release including the defendant's threat to public safety and the likelihood of returning to court.[1] The majority of the research on pretrial release however takes the form of quantitative analysis which identifies risk factors to predict a defendant's likelihood of re-offending (Austin, Krisberg, and Litsky 1985; Frazier, Bock, and Henretta 1980; Petee 1993; Sherwood-Fabre 1987). These studies overlook the cultural practices that shape how legal officials assess risk at the pretrial release stage and they focus primarily on "visible decision makers" (Petee 1993: 375) such as police officers and prosecutors. This chapter explores nonprofit caseworkers' evaluative tools for determining defendants' suitability for community-based supervision as well as the interviewing strategies they employed for assisting weak referrals and screening out problem referrals. The nature of these programs granted caseworkers a great deal of organizational autonomy to determine their client base and the county jail was a critical site where staff persons assessed inmates as potential clients.[2] Caseworkers increased the number of releases by facilitating interviews in a manner that directly benefited defendants who might otherwise remain detained without special advocacy. Carl's situation in the opening vignette also hints at how normal casework troubles constrained risk assessment practices to the detriment of arrestees. In the county jail, staffers' jobs were tantamount to working in a street level bureaucracy in that they evaluated inmates for pretrial release services in the face of limited time, short staffing, and heavy caseloads (Smith and Lipsky 1993). Defendants' self disclosures, in turn, revealed aspects of themselves that caseworkers labeled as evidence they were not amenable to community-based supervision. As we will read, nonprofits' screening practices were guided by a set of institutional parameters for measuring social worth as well as criminal risk which resulted in widening the release net for some and leaving others behind.

Interviewing as Storytelling

Caseworkers said they loved their jobs because they made a difference in people's lives, and they appreciated being part of an organization that advocated for alternatives to incarceration, mostly for poor, minority defendants. They frequently contrasted their jobs to those of bureaucrats who worked in government agencies. "All they do is push paperwork," said Staffer Mario Alvarez who worked at the Open Door after quitting his job at the Department of Public Health. He had had benefits and was paid well in that position. But he noted, remembering the incident with distaste, "When I first started, someone said, 'Welcome to the Department of Public Health. You're now part of the problem and not the solution.'" Caseworkers claimed that the mission of nonprofit programs, unlike government agencies, was to help defendants change their lives because they cared about people as individuals. Mario's pithy judgment is that "Bureaucrats only check boxes [but] we are not just filling a slot."

Staffers saw the defendant's potential for release differently than court officials and evaluated referrals through a multifaceted lens (Coutin 2000). In a fashion similar to Coutin's study of legal advocates for Salvadoran immigrants (2000), a kind of "double vision" was voiced by Reach caseworker Natasha Lee: "We read the rap sheet and we see what the defendant's record looks like and we personally talk to family members. We can see [the case] not just from a law kind of way, [but] a regular person kind of way." As evident in Carl's vignette, the jail interview is an important tool for assessing a defendant's suitability for release. At the core of their prescribed efforts to evaluate pretrial release petitions, staffers encouraged defendants to talk about their personal lives. The jail interview was an informal process to foster open conversational spaces and broad interpretations of defendants' suitability for community-based supervision. Caseworkers prompted defendants to talk candidly about their criminal history, how they supported themselves, personal and occupational aspirations, and private troubles that contributed to their cycle of arrests. A common sentiment among caseworkers was that good referrals saw their legal problems as a "wake up call," an opportunity to turn their life around, get off drugs, and find a job. Mario said to me: "[Defendants] in this agency need help, guidance, direction. The [criminal justice] system is a trap. They've fallen in. It's time to stop digging and think about how did I get in the trap, a reflective time." Open Door Supervisor Kelsey Martinez talked about interviewing as "less bureaucratic" and "less judgmental." "We talk to defendants and listen to their stories," she explained. For caseworkers, the general aims of interviewing as storytelling were trying to understand what led up to the person's arrest and how keep him or her from cycling through the justice system.

Caseworkers' jail screening practices were premised on the notion of what caseworkers called "listening beyond." During this narrative exchange, staffers gathered information to determine if the defendant was willing and able to abide by the terms and conditions of pretrial release. Supervisor Paul Lewis of Pathways said: "You have to listen, for me it's listening beyond. You learn what follow-up questions you need to ask. You are able to tease out lies or half-truths. A lot of people aren't giving the full story. They are embarrassed, or they think they will give the wrong answer." Listening beyond denoted good interviewing skills and was a sixth sense for discerning which defendants were likely to comply with the program. Listening beyond was also reflected in Second Chance worker Flamine Hernandez's statement, "A big part of [screening defendants] is trusting your gut." Similarly, Manuela Vega of Pathways decided against releasing a homeless person. She reasoned: "I just didn't get a good feeling about him." The method for evaluating referrals revealed caseworkers' tendency to base release decisions on their intuition and instincts that came from their learned experiences working with justice-involved persons. On the first day that I shadowed Open Door Caseworker Steve Brown to the county jail to conduct interviews he explained to me that he "knows" if a defendant is appropriate for his caseload "just by talking to him." "That's a skill and not everyone has it," he said.

Along these lines of listening beyond, Kelsey equated the interview process as solving a puzzle: "[Caseworkers] put together the pieces of a person's life. It's like trying to piece together a puzzle; the defendant's life is the unfinished puzzle. The job of caseworkers is to put the pieces of the person's life together to tell a story." Staffers often began the interview by saying "I'm here as your friend" or "I'm here to see if we can get you out of jail" as a way to ease into a dialogue about the defendant's background. Kelsey said pointedly during a caseworker training session that I attended, "Interviewing is an art form and style produces results." She continued:

> The purpose of the interview is to build a rapport with the [defendant]. You won't learn anything by just reading a person's rap sheet. It's important to make a personal hook with the client. Without the hook, you won't be able to make your client respond to you.

To make a hook, caseworkers listened beyond to gauge whether the defendant was either sincere or manipulative about getting help to change his or her life. Paul encapsulated the importance of listening beyond for evaluating good referrals for intensive, community-based treatment: "You want to pick the people that want the help versus the people that just want to get out." This was not an easy task.

Caseworkers' jobs involved face-to-face interviews with inmates and during this interaction they attempted to produce a certain emotional response, such as getting the defendant to express remorse for wrongdoing. Mimi Evans, a Reach caseworker, approached jail interviewing in a manner conducive to soliciting defendants' self disclosures. She said: "In the beginning, there's that tension, and I kind of want to calm it down, so I like to speak in terms to get him relaxed and speak up, because sometimes they hold back information." Similar to Hochschild's (1983) airplane stewardess, caseworkers regulated their emotional and interactional responses in ways that were consistent with larger organizational goals to gather sufficient information to assess their suitability for release. Although the majority of inmates cooperated and answered all the questions they expressed limited hope that their voluntary disclosures would help them get out of jail. Some defendants were reluctant to divulge personal information for fear of reprisal and shame. In particular, some individuals expressed concerns that caseworkers would pass on information about their private troubles to their family and friends who were called upon to act as references. Steve explained:

> That's one of the reasons I feel comfortable doing what I'm doing. I can break those barriers down because the trust issues are very important. [Defendant thinks] 'Why should I tell you? Even though you're telling me I can get out tomorrow, you expect me to sit here and tell you all my dirt?" "I'm a dope addict, I molested this child…' If they are not forthcoming, that will cost them the possibility of them getting out. So what? That's still not nothing. [Defendant thinks] 'If I give you that information, it still don't mean I'm going to get out. If I get denied, now you know my business, talked to my mama.'

And so, caseworkers judged defendants as potential clients by soliciting story telling yet the interview process represented some risk for defendants who elected to participate. Defendants then were expected to "act like clients" in a manner that persuaded the caseworker that they would abide by the conditions of their release. Listening beyond honed the skills of weaving the jail interview into a narrative fabric by asking questions to develop rapport, eliciting information, and ascribing meaning to defendants' responses. Staffers listened beyond for gaps or discrepancies, evidence of good or bad character, and degrees of commitment to change their lives. Interviewing as storytelling developed caseworkers' institutional parameters for assessing risk which, in turn, classified some defendants as worthy of special advocacy and others as potential trouble.

Strengthening Weak Referrals

In Jacobs (1990) book, juvenile probation officers spent time with cases that "attracted special advocacy" (103). Caseworkers' interviewing techniques reflected their inclusionary practices to increase the number of possible releases by providing particular judicial assistance to defendants who might otherwise be labeled as ineligible. Staffer Taj Ramirez of Second Chance explained how the program advocated for people by going beyond the routine way of compiling pretrial release petitions. He said, "The way the logic of the system works is, all you're supposed to do is the basics and let the judge do the math, but we do the extra stuff like a summary of the personal circumstances or history, stuff that would never make it into the bureaucratic way of doing it." Similar to Jacobs, I found that weak referrals were not atypical but rather commonplace and routinely problematic for caseworkers. A normal case for pretrial release is a person with strong community ties which are typically defined as a verifiable home address, a working phone number, good references, and some means of financial support (Ares, Rankin, and Sturz 1963; Austin, Krisberg, and Litsky 1985; Frazier, Bock, and Henretta 1980). Many defendants frequently fell short of this commonly held standard of a good risk. The defendant populations were characterized by high rates of underemployment and unemployment. Some defendants survived on small monthly sums from the public welfare system, including general assistance and social security benefits. Many defendants lived with and were supported by other family members, in particular parents and grandparents. Some defendants lived in single room residency hotels often located in high crime and drug trafficking areas of the city. Due to repeat arrests or substance abuse problems, defendants lost contact with or were estranged from family and friends. Caseworkers were compelled to advocate for persons with marginal eligibility in part because they represented the economic and social inequalities of the justice system. Steve said, "I've been through the system. I know the different elements that people have to go through on the street. It's tough sometimes to leave people behind that didn't have proper contacts." Caseworkers listened beyond and read between the lines of the investigatory materials to assess the true nature of individual risk and potential for community-based rehabilitation. This point was exemplified during my interview with Tracy King, an Open Door staffer. She said:

> I have gotten people who have had a long history of assault and battery but in their much younger years, like fifteen years ago. If it's cases like

that we take a look at them and take them sometimes. If a person has assault and battery, terrorizing and guns recently: no. But you know things happen in people's lives and they might be really, really in the [system] a lot and although they are still in the [system] they have changed, they are not doing the things they used to do. So, you look at that differently and try to give individuals a chance. Their [criminal] history may be "oh, no" but you still give them a chance.

Caseworkers labeled weak referrals as "wobblers." In the legal arena, wobblers are also a term to denote criminal activity that can be charged as a misdemeanor or a felony or the degree of seriousness based on the context of the alleged offense. In a comparable fashion, Second Chance Supervisor Mindy Demarco explained: "wobblers are people who are teetering between good risks and bad risks" because they do not meet the basic standards for pretrial release. Persons working in social service agencies produce rather than process clients in order to meet the programmatic expectations (Holstein 1992; Loseke 1992; Miller 1991). Caseworkers normalized interview techniques to provide special advocacy for weak referrals and packaged the investigatory materials into a strong petition for release. Second Chance staffers' decisions to recommend release, for example, were largely based on projecting how the bail commissioner would respond to the supporting evidence (see Emerson and Paley 1992; Emmelman 2003; Frohmann 1991). Caseworkers' influential power at the assessment stage stemmed from their complex position in relation to criminal offenders and court officials. They assisted defendants with crafting strong petitions that fit within negotiated benchmarks of a good risk in the broader courthouse community. Mindy stated, "[One of] the most important things about the interview is figuring out what the person is trying to accomplish. Are they trying to get their license back? If so, what are they doing to reach that goal?" The defendant's answers to these types of inquiries determined if the case had sufficient capital to be presented to the judge.

Consider Vince's case. Vince Reardon was a fifty-two-year-old African American man. Second Chance released him from jail in 1998; he had failed to appear in court. In March 2003, after Vince failed to appear in court to answer on library-related charges on three separate occasions, he was re-arrested on the active warrants. Since then he had been arrested at the public library on charges of public nuisance (sleeping under a table) and petty theft (taking someone's bag in the bathroom). Mindy decided to give Vince another chance because his latest FTA was three years ago. "Why didn't you show up for court?" she asked Vince, pointing out his most recent FTAs. Vince explained that he had been homeless off and on until six to seven months earlier. He had washed his clothes, and the little piece of paper with his court date on it was stuffed down his pants pocket. The paper emerged from the dryer in a matted ball. Mindy questioned him about the theft charge but Vince avowed his innocence: "I was in the bathroom and I put my bag on the floor behind me because the floor was wet. When I went to leave, there was another bag that looked exactly like mine and I picked it up by mistake." Mindy inquired, "Are you still homeless?" Vince explained that he slept in a small back room at Mission Hill Church in exchange for doing maintenance work and setting up the chairs for Alcoholics Anonymous meetings. He was on the waitlist to get into the church's shelter program. Upon hearing Vince's story, Mindy declared, "He's a wobbler." Vince did not "look good on paper" due to all his FTAs, his "story about missing court was shaky" and he "didn't really have a solid living situation." Vince had proclaimed his innocence of the alleged petty theft charge by stating that he "took the bag by mistake;" Mindy felt that Vince's explanation was not a reasonable way of explaining his arrest to Bail Commissioner Paul Krupky.

Caseworkers are skilled at weaving defendants' complex personal stories into simple legal accounts. For example, before Mindy could present Vince's case to Commissioner Krupky, she needed references to verify that he was indeed living at Mission Church. Vince gave Mindy the names of two people to call: Cora, the shelter coordinator at the church, and Anton, an old friend Vince had not spoken with in *years.* Vince did not know Anton's number but remembered he lived in El Torres, a neighboring town along the coast. Mindy reached Cora immediately and briefly explained that Vince was incarcerated. Cora confirmed that Vince had been living at the church for two months and was going to transition into the shelter program soon. Mindy expressed reluctance and prompted, "He needs to have a stable address to get out." Cora said, "It should count as a stable address. He'll be here at least another six months." Mindy then flipped through the phone book and was pleasantly surprised to find Anton's number listed. Anton confirmed that he knew Vince but did not know where he lived and had not seen him for some time but offered, "Vince is a good guy and he'll come back to court." Mindy felt better about Vince's case because she could present evidence of stable housing; she recommended him for release to the court and Commissioner Krupky granted it. The task of assisting weak referrals illustrates how caseworkers assembled information to cull together a good case for release (McConville, Sanders, and Leng 1991). The purpose of this strategy was to "close the gap" between the arrestee's questionable candidacy and the judge's expectations of a good risk (see Emmelman 2003). Similarly, in Emmelman's study of public defenders she observed that defendants' accounts of their personal lives and criminal pasts were often at odds with court officials' mainstream cultural values (2003). Here staffers attempted to enhance or improve upon aspects of the inmate's petition to secure approval from the court. I identified two "story-boosting" strategies that caseworkers employed to aid defendants who poorly construct their legal troubles as worthy of release (McConville, Sanders, and Leng 1991).

At Second Chance, one of the interviewing methods involved coaching defendants to provide reasonable explanations for why they failed to meet their legal obligations. Mindy explained, "Our job is to make their situation sound better than it is. Sometimes, I say [to the defendant], 'you're not going to get out. That's a lame excuse for missing court.'" Stan, a twenty-four-year-old Caucasian man, had been arrested for failing to appear in court to answer to two misdemeanor charges of illegal camping and drug possession. Stan explained to Caseworker Jordan Roberts that he occasionally camped near the corner of G and Caldwell, near the freeway on-ramp, with a couple of friends. When the weather was bad, he stayed with his mother and stepfather in a small room at the Pickering Hotel. Jordan asked him, "What should I tell the judge the reason you didn't make to court?" Stan admitted that he was scared about getting re-arrested if he showed up. Jordan explained to Stan that she had to "give the [bail commissioner] something better than that." At Jordan's prompting, Stan said that on the morning of his court date he had an appointment at Office of General Assistance in hopes of getting more stable housing. To overcome Stan's spotty criminal record, Jordan decided to capsulate his defense in the following way: he did not attend court because he did not want to miss his appointment to apply for benefits to help him get off the streets. On the elevator ride up the bail commissioner's chambers, Jordan added: "Judges love to hear that someone is getting their life together. That's music to their ears." Mindy, who accompanied us, concurred, "Judges like to hear [defendants] are bettering themselves. If you can give them one of those stories, it's always a plus." Stan's effort to gain stable housing was an understandable motive for missing his court date. He was approved for release.

As Stan's case illustrated, caseworkers bolstered weak referrals by prompting the defendant to explain why he or she missed court, what they are trying to do to take care of the legal matter, or the circumstances of the alleged crime(s). In response to this line of questioning, however, defendants often said: "I thought it (the case) would go away," "I didn't think I had to come back [to court]," or "I moved and didn't receive any notice." Caseworkers' experiences have taught them that these types of explanations amount to poor excuses and will not resonate well with the judge. Mindy said that arrestees commonly fail to appear to court for honest reasons. She said, "A lot of the time it's confusion [about the court system], that's the frustrating thing." Likewise, Natasha noted, "Sometimes it's difficult to get information from the defendant because they have trouble answering questions precisely. She explained, "[I ask the defendant] 'How long did you live in Los Angeles?' [The defendant will answer] 'A while.' [I will prompt] 'How long is a while?' "You have to press them to get something more exact." Mindy remarked on the subtle nature of coaching defendants as a mechanism for strengthening weak referrals:

> In reality, if they have a [bad] excuse for missing court, we try to help them work a better reason. [If they say] 'I was busy,' [we probe] 'what were you busy doing?' We try to tease out better answers.

Coaching better answers was a form of advocacy by educating the defendant about how the judge will likely view the strength and weakness of the case. The defendant, however, was also a culpable participant in constructing a viable petition. Mindy said, "The judge will ask me why this person did not show up [for court], so [the defendant] better come up with something good." She continued, "You know who [the judge] will let out, you know what to ask the client to up a defense in preparation to present a case. You need to be honest with the client about that." As a counter example, Mindy narrated how she did not present Tommy's case to the court because he "gave her nothing to work with" during the interview. She recalled:

> [Tommy] had 14601s [driving with a suspended license] from multiple counties and he failed to appear [to court] six times. I asked him why he failed to appear. [Tommy] said, 'I just didn't want to go' and 'I didn't feel like it.' He had nothing to work with. I kept telling him, 'I can present this to the judge, but he is going to say no unless you have better reasons.' He had terrible attitude about it. His attitude was such that I was sure he wasn't going to show up anyway.

Mindy explained that she "didn't even both to present him" to the judge. She justified this decision by laying claim to her legal authority, "I have to make the call. The judge is not there talking to the person, I am." Tommy's failed petition illustrates that defendants are burdened with overcoming caseworker mistrust and must utilize impression management strategies to convince caseworkers that they are committed to program compliance (Goffman 1959). Tommy's "terrible attitude" impressed upon Mindy that he was not entitled to be release and unlikely to come back to court.

Reach caseworkers' jail interviewing practices were also geared towards using story boosting strategies. Supervisor Stacy Abaya said to me during an interview, "we try to go the extra mile to help get defendants released." The organizational priority of Reach was to provide the courts with complete and accurate information to make informed pretrial release decisions. However, unlike Second Chance, because they did not orally present the case to the bail commissioner they advocated for weak referrals in a different way. Reach staff attempted to close the gaps between any discrepancies and missing information during the interview before the case was compiled on paper. On Wednesday morning, for example, Supervisor Rafik Nara was training a new employee. He emphasized heavily that bail commissioners liked to see things in chronological order. Rafik advised, "During the interview it's important there are no gaps [in the defendant's history]. Ask the defendant to clarify, if necessary." He continued, "If during the interview there is gap in where the person was living for, say, eight months, ask the inmate where they were living. They may say, 'Oh, I guess I was staying with my parents.' It then turns out he was homeless for those eight months. The [bail commissioner] wants to know all of that." Many defendants need special advocacy because they do not remember their previous address or means of support. As Stacy noted, "our population is not the kind to have planners and palm pilots to keep track of their lives." Due to the high illiteracy rate among the general jail population, some defendants do not understand what the word "previous" means and give the wrong answer.

Caseworkers' interviewing instruments however inadvertently weakened the defendant's opportunity to close gaps in their personal histories. Caseworker Bridget Milne was interviewing Darnell Stevens, a thirty-three-year-old African American man arrested on drug possession charges. He had moved to Washington, D.C. seven months earlier. For the past six months, he had been working as an information systems consultant in the capital city. Bridget asked, "How did you support yourself for the one month you were in Washington, D.C. before you got the job?" Darnell answered, "When I first got there, I worked at a temp agency." Darnell continued to explain that before moving back East he had worked as a web designer for a start up firm in San Miguel for five years, a high-paying job. Darnell's account of his work history in San Miguel and Washington D.C. suggested that he was a responsible and employable person. While this type of reporting enables the caseworker to accurately summarize the defendant's means of support, it is important to note that it is a snapshot in time, and depending on what scope of time that includes, the defendant may appear either more or less stable. The interviewing form requires the caseworker to document an arrestee's current and previous means of support, which in Darrell's case occurred only within the seven month period in Washington D.C. The bail commissioner was not informed of Darnell's five year job as a web designer in California. In addition, other potentially relevant information is not systemically reported which could leverage the petition. Darnell had a college degree from the local state university, but there is no question on the form about the defendant's educational background; it only gets reported in the comments section at the caseworker's discretion.

In most pretrial release programs, community ties are a critical factor for assessing the defendant's risk to public safety and the likelihood they will comply with the court mandates. One of the most important and challenging aspects of compiling pretrial release cases was verifying information and calling references. At the end of the interview, the caseworker asked the defendant to give them the names and phone numbers of friends, family members, or acquaintances. Calling on a defendant's references creates an immediate social network that would not otherwise exist. References serve: 1) to establish a character witness to see if a defendant is likely to come back to court; 2) to verify the defendant's address; and 3) to enlist the references as part of an informal social control network to help remind the defendant to attend all subsequent court dates. The inability to verify references however problematized caseworkers' efforts to screen referrals. Many defendants did not meet the threshold of good references and stable community ties that were required for release. Natasha explained this common problem:

> If someone is genuinely housed, like really has a place to live, it's not that difficult [to get references]. Sometimes, it's really difficult. Some people just don't have a lot of friends. Sometimes you run into the problem of all their phone numbers are on their cell phone and it's in [jail] Property or they have an address book and it's in Property. It's frustrating because they say 'I've got lots of phone numbers but it's in my property.' I say, 'I can't get your property.' They get frustrated because they might spend a night in jail just because they don't have numbers memorized.

In the Second Chance program, Max's situation reveals that because of defendants' tangential and tenuous relationships caseworkers are not always able to verify the defendant's social networks. Caseworker Flamine explained:

> [Max] owned a jewelry store but for some reason he had nobody with a phone that I could call or knew where he lived. Max gave me the phone numbers for the sandwich shop down the street and the antique store right next door. [The shopkeepers] all knew Max but they didn't know where he lived. I wasn't able to verify [his home address]. Sometimes things don't work out.

While Flamine did not present Max's case to the bail commissioner because it was too risky, caseworkers exercised their di*scretion to define* community ties broadly to accommodate persons without mainstream support systems. Marvin provides an example. He was arrested on multiple traffic violations. During his interview with Caseworker Mindy, he could only think of one person who might be able verify his address: his friend Randy. But Marvin did not know Randy's phone number or where he lived. They hung out together at the same neighborhood bar, The Eagle's Nest, at the corner of McGill and Canyon streets. The bartender was the only social link between Randy and Marvin. Mindy tells the story:

> [Marvin] said to call this bar [because] Randy hangs out there all the time. Randy might know where Marvin lives. I called the bar. The bartender knows Marvin and [Randy]. Randy wasn't there but [the bartender] called him on his cell phone. I called [the bartender] back; she gave me Randy's cell phone number. I called Randy and he gives the number for another person who knows Marvin's address.

Mindy enlisted the cooperation of Marvin's friends and acquaintances to help ensure he was eligible for and compliant with the conditions of his release. Caseworkers utilize a range of resources to strengthen a defendant's case for release. In Marvin's example, Mindy made his otherwise invisible social networks visible and presented them as credible evidence that Marvin would return to court. It is worthwhile to note that caseworkers not only cull together the good facts, but they also conceal the unfavorable particulars of the defendant's application for release. For example, the bail commissioner might be less inclined to approve Marvin's release if he or she knew that the defendant's primary social link was a bartender. Part of caseworkers' assumed responsibilities is to control information that may undermine the defendant's chances for release.

Weighing the Small Things

While caseworkers coached weak referrals using story-boosting strategies to help strengthen their petition for release, they also screened out problem referrals during the interview process. Mario advised, "You have to weigh the small things" in reference to the often fine line that separated weak referrals who were otherwise earnest about complying with the program and troubled cases who were manipulating the system. The small things were shaped in part by caseworkers' subjectivities towards defendants who cycled in and out of the justice system. "Reach is a privilege; it's not a right," asserted Stacy. Caseworker sympathy waned over time; the stress of jail work fostered a great deal of cynicism. Reuben Kiefer, a Reach staffer, said, "When I got here I felt sorry for [defendants], I believed everything they said. I was told I would get over it in two weeks." Caseworkers voiced that they were tired of seeing the same defendants arrested, released, and re-arrested again. Stacy coined the phrase, "different defendant; same story" because many inmates appeared to have similar personal and criminal justice backgrounds. She continued, "Sometimes I almost feel like I'm doing the same interview over and over again: drugs, family gave up on them." Caseworkers listened beyond for "red flags" (Ibarra 2005, 38) and white lies to indicate that the person was troublesome or apathetic.

Red Flags

A person's sense of privilege during the interview was an important red flag for caseworkers. Reuben said, "[Defendants'] sense of entitlement is off the charts. They feel...that society has shafted them so hard." Derrick Taylor who worked the swing shift at Reach said, "Some of these guys are a little flaky. [Defendants give excuses] 'It was my first time,' or 'I'm not a drug addict.' Sometimes it's better for them to be in jail." Caseworkers passed over defendants with bad attitudes, who swore, yelled, or acted inappropriately as personal affronts to their professionalism (Reich 2005). Samantha Green of Second Chance said, "I don't talk to people with hands down their pants." Caseworkers were less likely to legally assist defendants they labeled as failing to take personal responsibility for their criminal actions. Caseworkers were generally unsympathetic towards defendants who blamed the justice system, the police, or their spouse for their current incarceration.

References, in turn, also raised red flags by denouncing or disputing the defendant's candidacy for release. Under those conditions, the caseworker was indeed reluctant to go forward with processing the petition. Taj explained what he asks for and listens for when talking to a person's references. He said, "If I ask [a reference] 'if I let Charlie out, will he show up to court?' The person may say, 'Charlie is a junkie. If you let him out he's going to get a fix right away, he's never responsible.' I'm going to keep [the defendant] here because I don't feel comfortable [releasing him]." Caseworkers listen beyond by taking into account the personal views and experiences of the defendant's personal connections to inform the screening process.

Another red flag that caseworkers took under consideration was the degree to which the defendant demonstrated sufficient motivation to change his or her life. This was particularly apparent for the Pathways and Open Door agencies since they are intensive case management programs and the staff invested significant time and resources towards helping clients. Manuela explained, "Not a large percentage of people are able to get out because there is a certain caseload capacity. There's a lot more to trying to release them." Pathways Supervisor Dave Powell posed the question to new referrals about getting help in a straightforward matter. He said: "[I ask] 'are you interested in a caseworker?' and if [defendant] says 'I'm interested in whatever will get me out of jail.' That's not someone we really want to work with because they are not going to be able to hack checking in for six months and doing all these different things for the court." Dave highlighted the more subtle intricacies of listening beyond to determine if a defendant was motivated to get off the streets. He said during our recorded interview:

> It's a perception of whether that person is motivated. In jail, I think more people are motivated because they are good at convincing you. If someone has been using drug for thirty years and been living on the street for ten tells me, "I want to get a job and get housing" that's not realistic. Until you get treatment, you're not doing that [job and house]. If someone is trying to bullshit me or bullshit themselves, that's where I would say they are not motivated.

Interestingly, Dave suggested that if the defendant's expectations for changing his or her life are labeled as "unrealistic," it negatively impacted the caseworker's perception that he or she was truly motivated.

Listening beyond for red flags resulted in gendered release decisions because caseworkers attributed credible motivation differently to personal stories. Caseworkers encouraged defendants to talk openly about their private troubles, but they sometimes discriminated in the way they used those stories to make risk assessments. When women told stories about their children, they were often branded as selfish or bad mothers because they were using their kids to warrant caseworkers' sympathy to get out of jail. Stacy said, "I've heard defendants use their children as an excuse. [The defendant says] 'I really need [Reach]. I need to take care of my baby.' [Stacy responds] Well, where was your baby when you were out selling drugs to the cops? Right now you care about your kids but you didn't before." Stacy's statement echoed the sentiments of other caseworkers that defendants did not deserve to be released if they were not perceived as taking responsibility for their criminal behavior. Contrarily, when men told stories about their children, caseworkers tended to credit them as good fathers. This gender disparity in release recommendations appeared in the cases of Monique and Torres. On Monday, I accompanied Mario to the jail to watch him interview three new court referrals. We rode the elevator to the jail's fourth floor and entered the women's cell block. We approached the sheriff's deputy on duty, flashed our badges, and Mario said we were there to interview Monique Jones. The deputy nodded disinterestedly and directed us to a windowless room in the corner. A few minutes later, Monique knocked on the door. Mario motioned her in and directed her to take a seat in one of the orange plastic chairs. She shuffled towards us in her jail-issued slippers. Monique, a twenty-three-year-old African American woman arrested for conspiring to sell drugs, had been in jail for five days because she was unable to come up with a $5,000 bail bond.

Mario slid the interview form from the manila folder, introduced himself and said, "I was sent here by your public defender to see about getting you released and see if you're ready to deal with your issues." Monique nodded as tears welled up in her eyes; she mentioned her two-year-old daughter. "Am I getting out? I really need to get back to her," Monique pleaded. Monique's show of emotion did not appear to move Mario. Instead, it became a liability. Mario quickly issued a stern warning, "I don't want to hear you agree to anything just to get out. Open Door is an option and you don't have to take it." Caseworkers often said that defendants knew how to "manipulate the system." They strongly attributed their job success to their ability to be firm with defendants, "take control" during the interview, and not tolerate "their bullshit."

Mario began to ask Monique a series of questions in an efficient and direct manner: Where do you live? Does your family live near you? Monique told him that she lived in a small apartment with her daughter,

Rochelle. Her mother and sister lived in the same neighborhood and babysat while Monique worked as a receptionist for a social service agency. As Monique spoke, Mario wrote on the interview form. "Do you have any history with drug abuse and mental illness?" Mario inquired without looking at her. He glanced up when she failed to answer. Through more tears, she said "no" impatiently. She told us how her boyfriend used to beat her up, but she had gone to community college to better her life for her daughter. She planned to go back to school to get a good job.

The last set of interview questions asked about the defendant's criminal history: prior arrests, convictions, time spent in jail, or prison. Mario again warned Monique, "You had better tell the truth because [your] rap sheet is back at the office. If you lie, [my supervisor] will tear it up [waving the interview form]." Mario had no information on Monique's criminal history because the court had failed to provide it. Instead, Mario used the threat to persuade Monique to be "forthcoming" about her past. At the Open Door, an effective interviewing technique to solicit the truth was telling a lie. Monique claimed her innocence of the criminal charge and repeatedly told Mario that the police "just keep picking me up on [drug] conspiracy."

On our way back to the office, Mario said he would probably recommend Monique for release: "She was willing to get some help, so I'll give her a try." However, when we returned to the office, he grew increasingly uncertain about his decision. He pondered aloud, "I didn't like that she brought up her kid as a reason why she needs to get out [of jail]. Why didn't she think of her child before [she was arrested]?" Mario ultimately decided that Monique was "not sincere about turning her life around" and submitted a negative recommendation to the court.

Contrarily, Steve's decision to get Torres of out jail suggests that when men told stories about their children (which was less common), caseworkers tended to credit them as good fathers. He said:

Every case is different. I had a guy [Torres] who was married for five or six years. One night he had a little bit too much to drink, got into it with his wife, didn't touch her, made verbal threats. She got a stay away order, that's where he lives, that's where his kids are. He violated his stay away order because his kids said, "daddy, we miss you." He tried to sneak up and hug his kids and kiss them. The wife called in because he violated the stay away order. "[Steve], will you take him back" For hugging his kids? Yeah, I'll take him back. Even though he violated the stay away order, go by that house, I don't care.

These subtle forms of gender coding influenced release decisions. Steve morally justified his decision to accept Torres back onto his caseload because he labeled his illegal actions as "being a good father." Similarly, in Kleinman's (1996) study of Renewal, men who expressed vulnerability and emotion increased their status in the alternative organization (also see Lichterman 1989). Overall, listening beyond during the less formal interview process provided open spaces for staff interpretation of stories yet these interpretations created differences in assessment of risk and disparities in defendants' entitlement to pretrial release. Kelsey justified the agency's screening practices by saying: "Not everyone should be out of jail."

White Lies

Caseworkers were not only attuned during the interview for evidence that the defendant was not forthcoming but they also listened beyond to test whether the defendant was telling the truth. Caseworkers judged the veracity of arrestees' interview responses with varying degrees of suspicion. Reuben said, "Eight of the ten people I interview will deny [the crime]. The other two admit it. 'Attaboy, at least you told me the truth.' I'll respect him more." They claimed some defendants did not deserve to be released if they were making up excuses to explain the circumstances of their arrest. Kelsey warned of defendants' tendency to 'skirt the truth' during my caseworker training. It was caseworkers' jobs to help get the full story. She advised, "[Defendants] are not constrained by societal boundaries, so you must be firm." According to Tracy, this was an organizational necessity. She warned, "People have been through the system and know how to manipulate it. They know what to say." Along these lines, Anthony said, "I'd like to see the police report before interviewing someone to make sure [the defendant] is telling the truth [about their alleged crime]." In this example, he suggests that the police report is the arbiter of that truth and if the defendant is honest about the crime it is a positive indicator he or she is straightforward about other things and hence deserving of release. In Mario's words, these "small things" built up or broke down a defendant's petition for release in the screening assessment of the caseworker.

Caseworkers kept a watchful eye on defendants who might resort to trickery and manipulation to secure their release. As an example of a "white lie," Stacy explained, "Sometimes the defendant calls [the office] pretending to be the reference." Caseworkers grew wary of references if they sounded like they were coached by the defendant to say the "right" thing in order to verify the information. Steve described a similar problem of defendants in cahoots with family and friends on the outside. When defendants "rigged" references they called the family member or friend to forewarn them that someone from the Open Door will call to confirm a particular address. He said, "I know that they planned that. They had the opportunity to put that together. You know, so it's a give and take situation and I don't always think it's fair but it's out of my control." Again, the acquired skills of listening beyond helped caseworkers to determine when case information was legitimately proffered or a product of crafty deception. As evident in these examples, defendants and pretrial release staffers alike made use of the gaps and ambiguities in the screening process to control case information and influence the release decision.

Conclusion

This chapter analyzed caseworkers' practical understandings and interviewing strategies for assessing defendants' entitlement to pretrial release in the county jail. Judges and attorneys delegated their authority to nonprofit programs to help determine which defendants were appropriate for community-based supervision. The ways in which caseworkers evaluated risk contributes towards our understanding of how staffers used their gate keeping powers to selectively screen defendants as potential clients for pretrial release services. In particular, staffers blurred the lines between rights and privileges to assess defendants for ROR which duly influenced how they compiled petitions for judicial review. Nonprofits, as contracted entities, developed informal criteria to screen out defendants by drawing on their past personal experiences with clientele and taking into consideration limited organizational resources to meet the demands of growing caseloads. Caseworkers' definitions of risk were also influenced by individual perceptions and local agency cultures. Their decisions to recommend releases based on gut instincts for example suggests a certain degree of intangibility in terms of the criteria used to assess risk, which may contribute to incongruent release outcomes.

In total, the data showed that outsourcing judicial decision making to nonprofits both widened the net of possible releases and left people behind in jail. They evaluated defendants with a view towards maintaining their own standards of good risk while expanding the risk parameters to advocate for more releases. Caseworkers however earned reputations as good risk assessors because a great majority of defendants released into the community under their watch appeared for their court dates. These success rates in turn further enhanced the discretionary powers of outside providers. The next chapter reveals that staffers' screening practices were not autonomous from courthouse politics however. I explore the organizational level disputes and negotiations among caseworkers and court officials regarding what constituted pretrial release eligibility criteria. I also take the reader inside pretrial release agencies to explore how constructions of risk were contested internally and gave rise to competing ideals about the inherent value of casework. Nonprofit management scrutinized caseworkers' discretionary power to reject referrals and modified policies that contributed to higher rates of inmates denied entry into the program.

---

[1] 2009 California Penal Code - Section 1318-1319.5. Article 9. Procedure Relating To Release On Own Recognizance.

[2] Chapter two describes the referral and release criteria specific to each nonprofit program.

5

Judging Release Criteria

One afternoon, I accompanied Second Chance Caseworkers Mindy Demarco and Flamine Hernandez to present two release recommendations to Bail Commissioner Stephen Hayes. Flamine admitted that she did not feel comfortable presenting the first case, Ricky, and felt certain that the commissioner would deny her. Ricky Hopkins, a thirty-three-year-old Caucasian woman, had a "spotty criminal justice history and seemed really unreliable," said Flamine. She had failed to appear in court six different times. Sharon, the second case, had three failures to appear but Mindy recalled, "We had let her out before and she'd done really well. [Now] she was in a much more stable situation." Sharon however had been arrested in Alamo, a neighboring county, on other criminal charges. Once the case was resolved in the courts, the authorities transferred her to San Miguel to answer on the bench warrant case. Bail Commissioner Hayes denied Sharon and released Ricky, who, according to Flamine, "was practically homeless." After we left chambers, Mindy explained, "[Hayes] didn't know why [Sharon] spent so long in Alamo. He didn't want to let her out because maybe she had a really bad case. We don't have a really easy way of getting that information. We won't even know if he wanted to know that." She added, "The judges are somewhat unpredictable. You can have someone with one FTA on something stupid, like shoplifting and no new case and they say no for no reason. You have someone with six FTAs, and has multiple cases, clearly is on edge of being homeless and they let him out."

***

The previous chapter highlighted caseworkers' interviewing strategies for screening potential clients. I showed how staffers prompted defendants to tell their story and disclose aspects of the lives that caseworkers determined to be contrary with the expectations for program participation. These evaluative techniques also helped caseworkers to live up to the social justice goals because they benefited weak referrals or wobblers in need of special advocacy. This chapter explores the conditions under which court officials contested the release criteria that caseworkers used to determine a defendant's eligibility for community-based supervision. The cases of Ricky and Sharon reveal that caseworkers recommended releases did not always fit within the judge's parameters of a good risk. As we will read, bail commissioners held caseworkers to assumed cultural standards for presenting appropriate defendants for release and caseworkers had relative powers to respond effectively to allegations of putting forward bad risks. Judges and attorneys also attempted to expand the parameters by circumventing established protocols to get defendants into supervised release programs in spite of caseworkers' efforts to impose set criteria for the purpose of maintaining their agency standards. In turn, the principal guidelines for judging risk were also internally reevaluated by the nonprofit agencies to increase the number of releases and control caseworkers' discretion to reject referrals.

Negotiating Risk Parameters

The interagency relationships between bail commissioners and nonprofit personnel played a formative role in shaping pretrial release criteria in the courthouse community. For example, in the Reach program, caseworkers and court officials held competing views on the compilation of pretrial release cases and the interpretation of risk. Consequently few felony arrestees were released from jail on their own recognizance. Conversely, bail commissioners approved of the majority of recommended releases through the Second Chance program based primarily on caseworkers' recognized competence for presenting good risks, what French and Raven (1959) call "ritual power" yet court officials employed tactical methods to test caseworkers' reputed judgment.

Shifting Release Liability

Each day around noon, the Reach caseworkers on the day shift and the director sat down to lunch together in the break room. Natasha Lee, an employee, poked her head around the corner: "I'm going to walk this case over to Commissioner [Paul] Krupky." Stacy Abaya, a supervisor, joked: "Yeah, send him [the case] so he can get a quick denial." The room fills with laughter, followed by an abrupt silence. Rafik Nara, a weekend supervisor, threw up his hands in exasperation and said, in reference to the majority of arrestees denied release by bail commissioners, "The jails are overcrowded." No one responded; he continued, "Why doesn't the sheriff's department do something about it?" Stacy replied casually, "The sheriff's department doesn't say anything because if the jails are at capacity then they can ask for a bigger budget." Anthony Banks, a caseworker, jumped in and added, "The police can ask for a bigger budget because there are more arrests." Silence once again overtook the break room and the lunch hour resumed. The above vignette hints at the discordance between Reach workers and bail commissioners over the criteria used to judge the worth of a release petition. While Reach caseworkers limited their liability for release outcomes by not making recommendations and leaving the decision up to the court, they blamed bail commissioners' subjective standards for why a large percentage of pretrial release cases were denied. Bail commissioners, for their part, based release decisions in both legal and extra legal context and claimed that caseworkers did not provide them with adequate information to make an informed decision. This section explores how caseworkers and bail commissioners "shifted blame up and shifted blame down" to explain why arrestees were frequently denied release.

Reach caseworkers were duty bound to strictly follow the California penal code to determine which felony arrestees were eligible for release.[1] Paradoxically, bail commissioners expressed frustration with the types of cases that caseworkers sent for review. Commissioner Krupky claimed that [Reach] "sends anybody" for judicial review. He continued, "The [Reach] guidelines are broader and more liberal than I would like. They present cases with missing information and they also present cases with violent charges, domestic violence charges; I would never release defendants with those kinds of charges." In a similar vein, during an interview, Bail Commissioner Linda Delaney [said] she would never release [a person arrested for] a [drug] sells charge yet staffers subscribed to the notion that statute law determined a person's pretrial release eligibility. In light of the low percentage of prepared cases to approved releases, caseworkers claimed that bail commissioners failed to follow the law. Anthony said, "I think the judges need to be retrained on the parameters for release. There are actual (with emphasis) parameters, three FTAs, no violent cases, a release address. Those are all the parameters." Caseworkers were frustrated when a defendant met the basic statutory criteria for release and the commissioner denied their petition. Mimi Evans, a supervisor, claimed that Bail Commissioner Delaney "makes arbitrary decisions" and "uses her own parameters" when deciding whether to grant or deny releases. Mimi said in general reference to the disparate differences in who got released, "Two people were arrested for a vandalism charge. One was approved for release and another person was denied release." Similarly, Rafik said, "I would like to see the [commissioners] get together and decide on criteria that they think is most important and let us know. I wish they were a little bit more uniform in their decisions." Like Mimi and Rafik, other caseworkers felt that if the defendant met all the legal criteria, he or she should be released. During my interview with Anthony he said with a sense of dismay:

> There have been cases that I've deemed as being clean. The person has never been arrested before, the person lives at home and their mother or father verified the information and they still are denied. You'll get someone who maybe was shoplifting at Macy's but the person was never arrested before. I've seen them denied by Commissioner Krupky and Hayes.

In the day-to-day review of felony case petitions however bail commissioners relied on the use of their legal discretion to constitute parameters for making pretrial release decisions not legal statutes. Bail commissioners described the decision making process as "crafting a story" out of the case materials, "the ability to read between the lines" and "an application of judgment." The decision to grant or deny release emerged from a substantive review of the case including the arrestee's social, personal, and criminal justice history. While the defendant's criminal matter was the critical factor, commissioners also adopted a "relational orientation" (Conley and O'Barr 1990, 58) to their release decisions. They took into account the person's social standing in the community and how well they were embedded in social and familial networks (Conley and O'Barr 1990). For example, to make his decision, Commissioner Krupky read the reference report first to see what the family members told the Reach caseworker about the petitioner. He noted during our interview, "Sometimes the family members say, 'don't release him.' If the mother or sister says don't release him, they know him better than I." The strength of community ties is an important indicator yet many defendants qualify for public assistance programs, such as General Assistance (GA), Social Security Insurance (SSI), or Veteran's benefits. Commissioner Hayes said: "SSI or GA is almost as good as working at Bank of America for ten years. If you need your SSI check you're not moving to Canada tomorrow." In a manner similar to caseworkers' efforts to strengthen community connections court officials broadly defined social ties to reflect the general life circumstances of justice-involved persons.

Judge Richard Kwan said that when he presided over releases as a bail commissioner he looked for signs that the defendant displayed a clear pattern of "questionable behavior." He explained during our taped interview:

> The charges don't mean anything except that by statute some charges aren't eligible for Reach. Was the crime allegedly committed while the defendant was drunk? Are there discrepancies in the police report and the way his family and friends talk about him or her? Is the defendant 'laying claim' to something or someone?

Instead of judging the merits of the case on the arresting criminal offense, bail commissioners paid careful attention to the social contexts under which the crime was allegedly committed. Bail Commissioner Hayes stressed a similar point during our interview:

> You look at the charge and say 'this person is likely to get [released]' and then you look at the case and say thumbs down. [A] lack of community contacts or some other scenario has a much greater public safety quality to it. There are some cases that look really serious and the person has ties to the community and it's not a public safety issue.

In contrast to caseworkers' view that arrestees who have little or no criminal history should be considered good candidates for release, bail commissioners claimed that if the individual had a more extensive criminal history, it could benefit their chance of being released from jail. Commissioner Hayes explained the degree to which the criminal justice history informed his release decisions:

> The rap sheet can give you information. If there's no information on the rap sheet at all, it's a good thing they don't have a criminal history, but it can't tell you a lot. If the rap sheet says they failed to appear [to court], that tells you a lot. It may show that they made all their [court] appearances.

Persons with long criminal histories provide a wealth of information that enables the judicial officer to predict the future behavior of the defendant in terms of complying with court mandates if released into the community. Albeit counterintuitive, it might be riskier for the bail commissioner to release a person who has no criminal justice record. The bail commissioner's goal was to balance the defendant's presumption of innocence with public safety concerns and the odds of returning to court. The risk assessment decision was not based on a strict set of legal criteria but rather court actors applied the law based on information in the case materials.

Furthermore, bail commissioners' substantive orientation towards the law, and by extension the pretrial release criteria, conflicted with Reach's technology and methodology for assembling petitions. Caseworkers, who identified themselves as pretrial investigators, strove to report information to the court in simple, unbiased terms. Bail commissioners however wanted a narrative account about the person's life to get a sense of what motivated their criminality and potential for violence or likelihood of coming back to court. These storytelling markers were not easily accessible based on the way staffers' compiled pertinent information, which was detrimental to the person's chances of being released. If the cases contained missing or inaccurate information for example staffers stamped in block letters on the cover page "Unverified Information," "Discrepancies In Information" or "No Contacts." Natasha explained, "That's what makes the case accurate." Bail commissioners however relied on the cover sheet to quickly assess the merits of the release petition before reading the case contents. Yet as Anthony noted, "The cover [makes the case] look a lot worse than it is. Like a guy could have a lot of traffic convictions but the first thing the [commissioner] sees is four convictions." Bail commissioners asserted that they were operating at a disadvantage because they must make release decisions without speaking directly with the Reach caseworker. Judge Judith Fenton, who periodically reviewed cases on the weekend, noted, "[Reach's] work is sterile. [There are] three inches of report, no one's telling me something about the person, no one is telling me anything more than what is in [the] notes. So, I get a stack of papers." She refers to the Reach report as "sterile," yet caseworkers promote their practices as "objective." Similarly, Commissioner Hayes said, "The decisions that I make are greatly different than the decisions I would be making if I were the judge in the courtroom. I would have some personal connection to the defendant by saying 'I expect you to be here next week.'" In summary, adherence to formal law was the way that Reach caseworkers expressed their organizational values which conflicted with bail commissioners' reliance upon broader parameters to assess an arrestee's suitability for release. Judge Fenton's and Commissioner Hayes's comments suggest that assessing whether a person met the release criteria was produced through social relationships not bureaucratic files, a matter to which we now turn.

Testing Judgment

One afternoon, I observed Mindy and Jordan Roberts present cases to Commissioner Hayes. Towards the end, Mindy nudged Jordan to hand him a copy of the monthly March report. Commissioner Hayes took the report and, while scanning the figures, asked, "How are you doing?" Mindy responded casually, "It's the same as last time, ninety-two percent [of defendants appeared in court]. I'm working on the April report now and it will be about the same." The commissioner, seemingly pleased, replied with encouragement, "Keep those numbers up." These reports generated by the caseworkers not only showed that the agency was doing a good job getting defendants back to court, but that bail commissioners were approving the "right" releases. Second Chance's rates of success were quite high and crisp one-page reports were a powerful demonstration of caseworkers' skillful practices. During an interview with Mindy she explained:

> [Second Chance] has a reputation, a very good reputation; we do make good calls. If [the program] blows it off [presents bad cases], the commissioner will say 'you're bullshitting me all the time.'

As evidence of caseworkers' reputation as good risk assessors, bail commissioners Krupky and Hayes granted releases to over ninety percent of Second Chance petitioners. This high acceptance rate can be partially explained by the fact that caseworkers recommended low level offenders but staffers' technology for compiling cases posed a greater risk for the bail commissioner rendering the release decision than Reach. In the opening vignette, for example, Flamine could not provide Commissioner Krupky with information about Sharon's arresting charge in Alamo County because her access to legal documentation was limited to San Miguel County court records. Judge Kwan said of the Second Chance program, "They won't even have a police report. The judge is taking more of risk in making that decision but because it's misdemeanors it's not as bad of a risk." Even so, during an interview with Commissioner Hayes, he remarked: "[Second Chance Caseworkers] have time to pull the case together and it is culled together better [than Reach]." Commissioner Krupky echoed a similar comment during an informal exchange I had with him. He said, "[Caseworkers] are more careful [than Reach] about who they present to me." While caseworkers presented cases to the court with broader release parameters than Reach, they were also burdened with maintaining a trusting and credible reputation for getting defendants back to court.

Testing Judgment explores how caseworkers and court officials developed and sustained shared ideas about risk criteria. Commissioner Krupky said to me during the interview, "There is a mutual agreement about who is a good candidate. I know who I'll release and [Second Chance] knows who I'll release, so they bring me the best candidates. In honesty, most cases that come before me I release." The common release parameters were cultivated and continually negotiated during the everyday case presentations in chambers. This is exemplified by Flamine's experience when she was relatively new to the job. She presented Suzie's case to Commissioner Hayes. Suzie Howard was a twenty-four-year-old Caucasian woman charged with prostitution. Commissioner Hayes denied her release from jail because he had presided over Suzie's previous drug-related criminal case at the arraignment hearing, and he knew from experience that she would not come back to court. It was Flamine's first denial. She explained:

> Hayes didn't think Suzie would come back to court because of her drug use. I was very angry at the denial because [Hayes] made a decision without knowing enough and to prove a point. I think he trusts my judgment now.

Haas and Shaffir (1982) noted how medical students learned how to behave like doctors in order to be taken seriously by their peers. Commissioner Hayes did not believe Suzie would comply with court orders, but even more important, he needed to establish the parameters of a good case for release with Flamine, who was new to the job. Flamine has now been employed as a caseworker for a year and the vast majority of her recommended cases were approved for release. She noted with pride during our interview, "Hayes [is] impressed [with me]." Flamine's example illustrates that judging release criteria was linked to the bail commissioner's trust that the caseworker was operating within the negotiated parameters.

Testing judgment also refers to how bail commissioners closely monitored the compliance rates for some of caseworkers' recommended releases. Commissioners' "detective strategies" functioned as a test of the caseworker's judgment regarding which defendants were good risks. During my interview with Bail Commissioner Krupky, he introduced me to what he called his "little black book" in which he logged the names of defendants he approved for release but did not think would make it back to court along with the initials of the caseworker that recommended their release. Consider this example. I accompanied Caseworker Jordan Roberts to Krupky's chambers to present Marvin Leavy's case. Marvin was a twenty-four-year-old man who was arrested for failing to appear in court to face auto theft charges. It was Friday afternoon, which meant Marvin would not be due back in court until Monday. As Commissioner Krupky signed the release order, he quipped, "He has the whole weekend to forget about his court date but we'll give him a try." He then opened his black book and jotted down Marvin's name along with Jordan's initials. The fact that the case was approved for release suggests that the commissioner gave the caseworker the benefit of the doubt. A few days after the defendant was released from jail however he asked the caseworker whether the defendant came back to court. Commissioner Krupky expressed high regard for caseworkers' familiarity with their caseload: "If I want to know if a particular defendant went to court, I will ask the staff and they will know." Bail Commissioner Hayes also monitored releases, but because of his technical competence he was able to consult the court's database system to ascertain the information as opposed to asking caseworkers to update him.

Caseworkers played close attention to bail commissioners' monitoring practices and took the opportunity when questioned to "one up" the judge and demonstrate that the program's discerning release criteria effectively screened for good risks. On another afternoon in chambers, after Mindy presented Mike Handle's case, a thirty-six-year-old man charged with petty theft, Bail Commissioner Krupky took a moment to write down the defendant's name. Mindy asked, "Is there anyone else you'd like to know about?" Krupky glanced up momentarily and then consulted his list again. "Robert Jones?" he asked without looking up. "Yes, he came [to court]," she replied. Krupky nodded to indicate that he was impressed, "You guys are doing pretty good," he remarked as he crossed Robert's name off his list. "Either I'm not guessing correctly or you're doing a good job of getting them back to court." By offering to update the bail commissioner about the status of oth*er* defendants Mindy both appeared confident and revealed that she was well aware that he tested her release recommendations. The commissioner's response that he may not be "guessing correctly" could be construed as a humble acknowledgement of the caseworkers' judgment. This dynamic also suggested that caseworkers capitalized on opportunities to build their "risk reputations" through informal displays of competence and skill. A subtle display of power was evident since Commissioner Krupky keyed this monitoring practice as informal gamesmanship as opposed to asserting his legal authority to deny the recommended release. In spite of the more good-natured aspects of testing judgment, the social interactions were underwritten by an attempt to control the release criteria. The above examples illustrated that release criteria were constructed through rapport building between caseworkers and court officials.

In total, negotiating release parameters explored how the interagency relations between caseworkers and bail commissioners dynamically informed release criteria. Reach and Second Chance programs in particular revealed how trust, technology, and physical proximity were organizational features that influenced ROR decisions. I now turn to how judges and attorneys pushed to broaden the risk parameters by referring defendants who did not meet the program's criteria.

Regulating Referrals

Pretrial release referrals are rooted in what Emerson and Messinger (1977) called the "micro politics of trouble." Court referrals to nonprofit programs by their nature indicate that the defendant is causing problems and disturbances in the community, the jail, and the courts (Emerson and Messinger 1977). These referrals that are passed onto caseworkers then pose some potential trouble in terms of the agency's cultural standards of a good risk and available organizational resources to meeting the potential client's needs. To manage caseloads, they enforced established release criteria and standard legal protocols to keep unsuitable, court-referred defendants off their caseloads. I explore judges' and public defenders' unregulated methods for sending referrals and how caseworkers usurped the power of the court by denying, what they considered to be, inappropriate defendants entry into their programs. Caseworkers in effect ferreted out problem referrals by detecting court officials "real reasons" for sending them (Emerson 1991, 198).

Judges and public defenders, as the principal referral agents, sent many misdemeanor and felony defendants to supervised pretrial release programs, namely Pathways and Open Door, during the pretrial proceedings in hopes of freeing up jail beds, reducing caseloads, and getting defendants into treatment. Open Door Supervisor Lee Mitchell surmised, "It's relatively easy to get referred [to the program], but much harder to get in." Regulating referrals suggests that caseworkers evaluated defendants with a qualitatively different set of criteria than court actors. To the dismay of judges, caseworkers rejected many defendants in spite of the will of the court to release them. While Judge Kwan supported the programs, he noted that they operated quite independently and suggested that the courts should play a larger role in dictating how they function in the justice system. For example, he echoed a general sentiment among the judiciary that the release decision should rest with the court, not the caseworker. In his chambers one afternoon, he spoke of his preference to simply send, not refer, defendants.

> [Caseworkers] make [their] own decision whether or not they can handle the individual. We [do not] send [defendants]; [the program] accepts them or not. In many cases, I've requested [a] review and its come back negative, they would not accept them. The determination is made by [caseworkers] of 'can we handle this person?' That's a big difference.

Courtroom judges then had less power to move defendants into pretrial release programs because caseworkers declined to accept them onto their caseloads. Wayne Brooks, the Open Door director, described this problem as: "Judges take advantage of the program and they interpret the program differently [than caseworkers]." Judges, as well as, attorneys also made referrals to the Open Door beyond the stated criteria as part of a larger shift towards placing offenders into treatment facilities as well as reducing the jail population. Supervisor Kelsey Martinez explained:

> The system is really pushing to find slots for inmates in programs. Judges are referring defenders for lesser and lesser mental health diagnoses, like depression. Judges see this as an opportunity for program placement. We are also getting referrals for people accused for more serious offenses, murder, violent crimes. Crimes we would normally never consider.

Caseworkers also claimed that court officials frequently referred defendants who were habitual offenders or unlikely to meet the terms of their release into the community. Paul Lewis, a Pathways caseworker, explained:

> A lot of homeless clients have been referred by lawyers or judges. Usually the lawyer referrals are people who are difficult. A lot of times people have mental health issues. Judges refer defendants who have long histories of [court] non-compliance and more serious misdemeanor offenses, like assault and battery.

As a consequence something tantamount to "referral ricochet" was commonplace as court actors referred and re-referred defendants who did not meet criteria and failed to comply with the program once released. Caseworker Steve Brown of the Open Door explained:

The court [thinks] if [the defendant] is not a threat to the public then [the program] should take them. The court doesn't care if he doesn't have an address or if he ran away from [the program]. In the interview he lies, he's not forthcoming, so I deny him. He goes to court and they send him right back. It happens all the time.

According to caseworkers, the court also sent unregulated referrals to pretrial release programs to solve other types of institutional problems (Emerson 1991). Kelsey and I left the Open Door office, walked across busy Miller Avenue, and climbed the courthouse steps on our way to deliver a report to Judge Roberta Small in chambers. Judge Small handed Kelsey the referral paperwork for a felony defendant with a long record of non-court compliance. She said with a hand wave of indifference. "I know you won't take this client but I'm referring him because I want to shut up the attorneys." Wayne pointed to another example of how the court "took advantage of the program" when judges began to funnel cases placed on the Drug Court waitlist to the Open Door for interim supervision. On a Tuesday afternoon, Rebecca Peters, a public defender in Judge Neil Evan's court, entered the Open Door office, approached Lee and handed him a thick file. "Could you guys babysit someone who's on the Drug Court waitlist?" she asked. "The judge wants the defendant to have something to do." Lee leafed through the case and begrudgingly said he would consider it. As evident in this example, it was to the public defender's benefit to develop stronger network ties with the staffers; they made an effort to visit the nonprofit office to make specific or unusual requests that might otherwise be denied if left to the bureaucracy of routine court processes.

Caseworkers deployed several tactics to refuse court referrals they labeled as "not program amenable" by enforcing the release criteria and the edicts of legal procedures. Open Door caseworkers mandated discovery materials (the police report and defendant's criminal history) from public defenders to make referral assessments and Reach caseworkers denied attorneys access to case materials short of following procedural law. For example, one morning, a public defender entered the Reach office. He explained to Stacy he was the "lead attorney" for his client, a thirty-four-year-old woman arrested for felony grand theft. He requested a Reach workup. The workup is the local programmatic term for the pretrial release case materials that caseworkers compiled for the bail commissioner. Stacy, sensing where the attorney was going, advised him: "We don't recommend [defendants for release]." The attorney jerked back in surprise and then responded, "Oh, what *do* [with emphasis] you do then?" Stacy explained their services and then informed him that, due to discovery laws, she could not release the defendant's file to him. The attorney was lawfully bound to request the file in open court with the judge and prosecutor present. The attorney took out his cell phone and left a message to the recipient relaying this information. He left the office and said he would back in touch. This example highlights a couple of key points. Reach caseworkers enforced court protocols by citing the discovery laws; the attorneys were either ignorant of this decree or they tried to circumvent procedures in the interest of time or as a tactical move to best advocate for the client.

Similarly, Open Door caseworkers accused public defenders of thwarting the referral process by withholding discovery materials due to concern that the program would reject the defendant due to their criminal history. The attorney's failure to provide the necessary documents resulted in procedural delays. Kelsey said, "Referrals without discovery are put over for a day." She continued, "It is very difficult to get discovery materials. It's been a long time battle. Sometimes we have the make release decisions based only on the interview data." This power struggle was made apparent to me when I followed Kelsey into Judge Kevin Mahoney's courtroom for a pretrial conference. The courtroom was empty except for the judge, the prosecutor, public defender, and the bailiff. Kelsey approached the bench to join the discussion about a defendant who was referred to the Open Door for intensive mental health treatment. Kelsey knew of the case immediately and asked the public defender for discovery on the case. The attorney's response was plainly agitated: "What do you need it for?" Kelsey replied with a cool demeanor: "We can't make any decisions about the case until we have discovery." The public defender said she was frustrated because the referral was taking a while. Kelsey assured her that once they had discovery, they could proceed with the assessment. As we turned to leave, the judge asked Kelsey, "Are you part of any other cases." Kelsey replied no and the public defender said, "I wish she was, she can tell us all what to do." The relationship between caseworkers and public defenders is complex. These examples demonstrate how caseworkers act in a judicial fashion by demanding discovery before rendering a case decision. It is important to note that defense attorneys relied on pretrial release staffers to get their clients out of jail; the personal information obtained by the caseworkers' interview assessment is also used as leverage for the public defender in court to build a legal defense for their client. Conversely, caseworkers' pervasive powers also undermined the attorney's efforts to control the direction of the case, as Kelsey's exchange illustrates.

Second, caseworkers regulated referrals by refusing to conduct interviews with defendants who did not meet the release standards. The criteria established by the Open Door for example disqualified defendants if they were charged with any crime of violence, including possession of a deadly weapon, sexual assault, arson, or kidnapping. Some court referrals, however, did not meet these basic conditions. Caseworker Tracy King said:

> When you get clients that are basically drug related, petty theft, vehicle code, stuff like that we have a large acceptance rate. Lately, we've been getting a lot of garbage. I don't mean to say [defendants] are garbage but people that have a lot of batteries, guns, you know, violence. We have a tendency to deny a lot of them.

Caseworkers screened the referrals carefully because, at times, public defenders "downgraded" the criminal charge on the referral form to better the chances of getting the defendant out of jail. The problem of public defenders "sneaking charges" past caseworkers is illustrated by Frank Holmes, who was referred from Judge Herbert Mill's courtroom. Lee rushed into the Open Door office around eleven am to drop off six new referrals. Tracy shuffled through the carbon slips then stopped and peered closely at one of them. It was a second degree burglary. Tracy asked me to check the court management system on the computer to see if that was correct because "sometimes public defenders change the charge because they know Open Door won't take the client otherwise." I checked the system which listed that Frank Holmes was charged with a first-degree burglary. Tracy said aloud, "We don't take first degree burglaries." She returned Frank Holmes' referral to court the next day with a brief memorandum stating: Not considered because of the charge. "Not considered" was a frequent label for rejected referrals. During an interview with Steve, I asked him what this meant. He explained to me: "Not considered means you don't have to interview the referral. That's a decision that caseworkers can make." Steve went on to say that a referral with a history of noncompliance is also sufficient grounds for not being considered by the program.[2] He explained:

> I got a [court] referral today for this guy who was unsuccessful the first time we had him. He was referred [from court] and he was not considered; we feel that's fair. If you did bad [before] nine times out of ten, [you're] not going to be considered. He was here three months ago and he came to the office one time. What has changed in the last ninety days for me to want to take him?

For caseworkers, "not considering" a referral approximated a face rejection of defendants who do not meet the basic criteria for supervised release.

A third strategy that caseworkers used to turn away bad referrals was conducting a "courtesy interview." Here the caseworker goes through the motions of interviewing the defendant to appease the referral sender but with the full intention of issuing a denial. Judge Will Hwang referred Barry Jones, a forty-one-year-old African American man, to the Open Door. After perusing Barry's file, Mario complained to his supervisor, Lee, that the defendant should not be considered (meaning not get an interview) because he had "too much violence in his past." Barry's petition for release was rejected and sent back to court. The next day, Judge Hwang promptly re-referred Barry to the program for further consideration. Lee directed Mario to do a "courtesy interview," meaning he should interview Barry just to satisfy the judge and issue a second denial to ward off further requests.

While judges and public defenders took exception to caseworkers' high rejection rate of many referrals, they softened their protests in the form of making personal appeals to caseworkers. Caseworkers, *as* contracted agents, deferred to the judge's orders. As Mario explained, "Sometimes the judge will tell the court team members that [he or she] wants someone [out] specifically. We never say no to a judge." On one occasion, Laney Everest, the Pathways director, and I were compiling the program's quarterly progress reports in her nonprofit office located six blocks from the courthouse when Judge Scott Edwards called her on the phone. After she hung up she explained to me that the judge asked her to accept a defendant into the program. Shelly Nealon, a thirty-eight-year-old Caucasian woman, had a drug possession case in Edwards' Drug Court and she was currently in a stable recovery house. However, another citation (for a separate criminal case) had just been issued and she would soon be re-arrested. Judge Edwards feared that this impending arrest would derail her rehabilitative progress at a local recovery program for women. The judge hoped that Laney could facilitate the process by accepting Shelly into the program, get her back on calendar to shield her from the bench warrant, ensure that she attended all subsequent court dates, and completed her drug treatment program. Laney agreed to look into it once she arrived at the jail in the afternoon. She hung up and said she knew the woman: "She's crazy, really crazy." In a similar vein, Caseworker Jorge Garza of Pathways entered Judge Fenton's chambers to deliver a progress report on a homeless defendant. The judge listened intently and, before he left, made a new referral: "I want Mr. Deacon to try to go through your program."

Re-referring defendants was one method that court officials used to appeal denials. Public defenders also made unannounced office visits and phone calls to sway caseworkers to consider releasing their clients. On one such occasion, Jeff Snow, a veteran public defender, entered the Open Door office. He approached Tracy and asked why she had denied his client, Malcolm Smith, for release. Tracy, recalling the case immediately, said, "He was denied for lying about his past violence." John stated in defense of his client, "Oh, he didn't understand what you meant by past violence." He asked Tracy if she would reassess her decision if Judge Mahoney issued a re-referral. Tracy reluctantly agreed. In another example, Susan Higgins, a public defender, entered the Open Door office to inquire about her client who had been denied release. She approached Mario and held up a copy of the denial form. She said, "[the report said] his address was unverified but I called the number and confirmed the defendant lived at the address. I thought that was why [the defendant] was denied." Mario entered his cubicle and tapped at the keys to pull up the case management notes in the database. He told Susan that the defendant was released to Open Door back in March of 2002 and he quoted the case notes, "he was not program amenable because he left the program without authorization." Susan attempted to promote her client's potential as a good risk, "Maybe the client has changed, that was back in March." Mario assented to interview the client if the re-referral was formally processed by the court.

As these examples suggest, public defenders were influential players in the referral process and caseworkers faced increasing pressure to yield to their requests. Lee stated, "Public defenders will coach defendants to say yes to everything [Open Door] says to help them get out." He explained during a staff meeting that public defenders know that caseworkers are most likely to recommend release if the defendant demonstrates a willingness to get treatment, such as drug counseling. Similarly, Kelsey spoke of public defenders' increasingly clever means to get their clients out of jail. At case review one afternoon, she said to the staff:

> Public defenders only worry about getting their client out, that's their job but that's not always a good thing. If the client is denied release through Open Door, then the public defender will ask that the defendant be assessed for mental health problems two days later. Public defenders have figured out that their clients have many options.

Both Kelsey's and Lee's remarks suggests that public defenders' zealous legal advocacy for their clients exacerbated the referral problem for caseworkers.[3] Public defenders wanted to get the defendant released from jail under most circumstances and since that decision rested squarely with the program staff, the attorneys made special efforts to appeal to them. Lee explained that public defenders have "profiled caseworkers so they have a pretty good idea of who is most likely to get their client out."

To further demonstrate this point, public defenders also typed up special memos to build a persuasive case for supervised release. Stephanie Bellows, a public defender, wrote the following memo to Lee about her client, Michael Thomas, along with the referral slip issued by Judge Herbert Mills.

Judge Mills ordered an Open Door report for Mr. Thomas [defendant]. Mr. Thomas was at General Hospital for a knee injury and is alleged to have struck his doctor there when the doctor tried to wake him up. Mr. Thomas is participating in [a Veterans program]. He is HIV positive. He says he has some kind of prescription and thinks he may have taken too much on the date of the incident [alleged crime]. I'd like to release him so he can keep working with [the program] and keep that bed.

The information in the memo read as a descriptive account of Mr. Thomas' case but Stephanie also used language to frame Mr. Thomas' criminal activity as potentially accidental in that it occurred in a medical setting while the defendant was recovering from surgery. The alleged assault quite possibly was caused by Mr. Thomas' negative reaction to the medication legally prescribed to him. The attorney situated Mr. Thomas in a sympathetic light by mentioning his HIV status and, in turn, illustrated that public defenders were attuned to caseworkers' preferences for clientele that are willing to participate in therapeutic interventions, such as the veteran's program. As was evident in the courthouse community, the ways in which actors talked about the worth of a case reflected an ongoing process of organizational learning among outside providers and traditional court functionaries regarding jail alternatives. As we will see in the next chapter, public defenders efforts to advocate for referrals mimicked caseworkers' story telling techniques to bring about judicial clemency.

And so, Open Door and Pathways staffers in particular assumed a judicial role and used their gate keeping powers to filter out many court referrals they labeled ineligible. Paradoxically, fewer defendants were granted release by caseworkers than either the courts or the sheriff's department would prefer.

Internalizing Accountability

In the 2009 Pretrial Justice Institute survey, the American Bar Association (ABA) and National Association of Pretrial Services Agencies (NAPSA) encouraged pretrial release programs to develop their own risk assessment standards based on local research. As we read in chapter four, caseworkers generally eschewed standardized assessment tools in favor of individualized and therapeutically based criteria for evaluating a defendant as a potential client. Nonprofits, as contracted entities, were not necessarily beholden to exacting standards for judging program eligibility. As Open Door caseworker Vince Smith said during a recorded interview: "We are not controlled, wholly by the government and their standards; it gives us flexibility to address issues in a way that we see fit...as opposed to being driven by these direct parameters." Inside the pretrial release agencies caseworkers were cognizant that routine pretrial release decision making practices created incongruent outcomes. Internalizing accountability investigates how nonprofit agencies scrutinized jail screening practices and analyzed organizational level criteria to increase the number of releases.

During a quiet Friday afternoon at the Open Door, I overhead Mario and Tracy talk about how the program director was concerned that the number of new court referrals were low; the previous month was also the lowest number of release recommendations. As I learned through office talk, the supervisorial staff sensed that the nonprofit had earned a reputation among judges and attorneys for issuing denials; the county sheriff and the courts pressured the agency to take on more clients. The problem of "too many denials" was also the subject of whispers within the agency that rose quickly to the surface of open debate. Victor said to me privately, "Sometimes I get the feeling that [caseworkers] look for reasons to deny rather than to accept clients for services. I think they get a wave, a huge number of referrals and they have to be discerning, there's the reputation of the organization at stake, you can't just take everybody out of jail." The Open Door took inventory of their internal decision making processes as a means to pressure caseworkers to base their referral decisions more on objective criteria. Lee offered some institutional history on the criteria for making release decisions. He said:

> We used to use a pros and cons sheet to decide whether or not to take a client. But now the decisions are made by the values of the

caseworker, which is much more subjective. We need a systemic decision making process that will hold us accountable internally.

In an attempt to control caseworkers' blanket discretion to evaluate defendants' suitability for supervised released, the Open Door instituted daily case review meetings during which the collective staff was encouraged to challenge and deliberate individual referral decisions. The case review meetings were part of a larger shift in the agency to advance organizational tools and teach caseworkers to closely scrutinize each other's release decisions. Lee described case review as an opportunity for supervisors "to give caseworkers direction and increase levels of awareness [and] convey what the court is looking for in a case." Vince said, "[Before case review] caseworkers let each other go blind, we would never let a client go blind." The forum was a venue for providing feedback, guidance and redefining risk to get more people out of jail. Disparate release decisions among the staff were shrouded by local programmatic terms to classify their decisions to reject referrals such as "not considered," "not forthcoming" and "not program amenable." These labels came under examination to "detect the real reasons" that caseworkers refused to accept the client (Emerson 1991, 198). Vince explained, "They are now buzz words that may be okay to use in court because we don't want to prejudice the judge by saying too much about the client but those terms are in need of internal scrutiny, we need meaning attached to them." Paula Davis' referral provides a case in point. On a Wednesday afternoon, Kelsey led case review and tapped at the keys on her laptop. Paula's file popped up on the large white screen. Mario interviewed Paula, a thirty-nine-year-old Caucasian woman, in jail earlier that morning. She was charged with felony drug possession of marijuana. Mario rejected the referral and classified Paula as "not program amenable." Kelsey asked Mario to explain why he denied her release considering her criminal charges were for nonviolent offenses. He said, "She said she has a legal right to smoke pot [due to medical problems] but she was caught with two little baggies of pot in her baby's stroller." Vince leaned forward and questioned his reasoning, "So you're making a moral judgment about the pot in her baby's stroller?" A discussion ensued and in light of Vince's protestations, Mario assented to take Paula onto his caseload. "Okay, okay," he said holding up his hands in capitulation.

Paula's example reveals the tension between caseworkers' values-based recommendations and the agency's efforts to objectify release decisions as a means to increase the number of recommendations. Lee surmised, "There are lots of gray areas [in making decisions] and caseworkers need to make more progressive decisions." These "grey areas" were distinctly patterned around gender and race differences in release recommendations. Researchers have certainly documented racial disparities in sentencing decisions. Bridges and Steen (1998) studied the mechanisms by which probation officers assessed Caucasian and minority juvenile offenders contributed to racial disparities in sentencing recommendations. Albonetti and Hepburn (1996) studied whether the prosecutor's decision to divert a felony drug case into treatment is informed by "the defendant's ascribed and achieved statuses" (64). Demuth's (2003) research on pretrial release decisions also found Hispanics were least likely to benefit from OR release. Caseworkers made allegations of racial disparities to expose and break down subjectivities towards black and Latino defendants in particular. Tracy joked to me during a lull in office activity, "Mario takes everyone as long as they are Latino." Mario denied the accusation and expressed concern that I would take her remark seriously. Perceived racial disparities were again discussed during my interview with Steve, "Latino clients are treated better than blacks and blacks have been made to do more rigid programs [if released]," he said. Beneath the gender and race problem was the core tension between caseworkers' values-based assessments and the agency's efforts to standardize release criteria. Tracy said to me during our interview:

> Don't get me wrong. I'm not a racist; I'm not prejudiced. When a client has been here two days from another country, comes here to sell drugs and I'm getting him out because I feel sorry for him versus someone who has been here all their life, same situation, denial. To me, I don't like that. That bothers me. I think if we had more of a protocol to follow of who can get out and why they can get out; I think it would be better. Not because I feel sorry for a client do I get him out.

Internalizing accountability also refers to how caseworkers modified release criteria because many potentially good clients did not meet the basic qualifications. In chapter four, the practice of strengthening weak referrals reflected this larger organizational problem. Mindy said: "We are worried about our numbers. They have been low because of the criteria; many people don't qualify for the program, so the numbers are low. Sometimes you can find a way around it but sometimes you can't." Second Chance and Reach caseworkers changed their organizational policy by reducing the number of required references to be eligible for release. Historically, pretrial release programs commonly mandated that defendants provide three verifiable references in order to secure release.

As a remedy, caseworkers decided to present cases to the bail commissioner with only one reference. Mindy justified this policy shift by citing what she assumed to be court officials' unawareness of how the program worked. She said, "The bail commissioners really don't know about the number of references. The number of references is more an internal thing," she explained. The shift from three to one reference went against the purposes and intent of pretrial release which is based on the assumption that broad social networks will help the defendant to comply with court mandates. The Reach staff also adapted their reference policy to increase the number of releases but for reasons that fit their organizational values. Supervisor Stacy explained that they used to require three references but they changed it to one. Oftentimes, she explained, a defendant gets one good reference that verifies all the necessary information but the other two references provided conflicting information, which is a detriment to the defendant. Stacy summed up, "If we get a good reference after the first call we stop. If the first call is not a good reference, we keep going" [meaning call the other two references]. This policy shift also revealed the organizational limits on caseworkers' time and resources influenced release criteria. It was very difficult to contact references to verify information. Many times, the phone numbers that defendants provided were incessantly busy or disconnected. Overall, modifying the program guidelines increased the number of referrals and releases but also risked the possibility of increasing the number of persons who failed to appear for court. Nonprofits' reputations at the Hall of Justice hinged on court officials' perception of its staff as good risk assessors. And so, they adjusted policies to advance their progressive agendas but with a critical eye towards maintaining a low failure to appear rate.

Conclusion

Judging release criteria illustrated that caseworkers and court officials alike faced institutional pressures to reevaluate OR criteria for purposes of controlling the numbers and types of defendants granted community-based supervision. In doing so, they routinely based their pretrial release decisions on criteria that fell outside of the boundaries of statute law. Caseworkers held traditional justice actors accountable to their release standards with a view towards maintaining their own standards of a good risk and to ensure the integrity of their programs. Overall, caseworkers keyed the iron cage by regulating and deregulating release criteria which exemplified their lawful authority without formal enforcement powers. Court officials, however, developed inventive ways to push the official parameters of the worth of a case to get more defendants out of jail. In total, judging release criteria was co-constructed between outside providers and traditional court functionaries in ways that widened and narrowed the release net. In the next chapter, caseworkers used rhetorical strategies to bring about court alterative outcomes by transforming how traditional court officials interpreted the nature of the defendant's criminality. We will also read that presentation style in courtroom settings was a critical aspect in shaping legal decisions (Conley, O'Barr, and Lind 1978). Caseworkers, as assistants to the defense, employed evidentiary tactics and staged performances to bring about an alternative disposition in the courts.

---

[1] Reach only presented cases to the bail commissioner that met the minimum legal standards for pretrial release eligibility. Second Chance, Pathways, and Open Door developed particular criteria for program participation in conjunction with the courts and the sheriff's department.

[2] This information is available in the discovery materials or the court management system.

6

Assisting in the Defense

On Monday morning, just before nine, the courthouse was abuzz. I waited for Jorge Garza, a Pathways caseworker, near the first floor elevators. Jorge arrived minutes later flashing his security clearance card to the sheriff deputy on duty and avoided the long line to pass through the metal detector. He signaled to me to take the stairs and we rushed to the second floor in search of Ron Carillo, a homeless client. Jorge was relieved to see him sitting on a long bench outside Judge Edwards' courtroom. Ron looked glum; he was hunched over and ran his fingers nervously through his mop of dark hair. Ron, a thirty-eight-year-old Caucasian man, had been addicted to methamphetamines for five years and spent frequent stints in jail on possession charges. After five years of using, his five foot ten inch frame was starkly thin and his skin tone ashen. Homeless for eight months, Ron agreed to enter an inpatient substance abuse program. "How ya doing, man?" asked Jorge in a jovial tone, giving Ron's shoulder a squeeze. He escorted Ron into the courtroom, seating him near the rear doors. "I'll be right back," he said. I followed him as he approached Lisa Young, the public defender, at her seat near the front of the courtroom to discuss the possibility of referring Ron to drug treatment. Ron had been mandated to substance abuse treatment twice before, but had dropped out both times; Lisa shook her head in doubt, telling Jorge that given Ron's track record, the district attorney would "put up a fight" but she agreed to give it a try.

Moments later, Judge Phillip Edwards emerged from chambers and took his seat on the bench. Ron's case was called and Jorge summoned him to the podium. Lisa formally requested that Ron be re-referred to drug treatment, this time under the supervision of the Pathways program. The prosecutor strongly opposed, citing Ron's failure to "take advantage of repeated offers by the court to get treatment." Edwards pondered the impasse and then asked the prosecutor, "Was Jorge involved," alluding to Ron's past referrals. "No, I don't believe so, Your Honor" he answered hesitantly. Edwards smiled and granted Ron a re-

referral to a substance abuse program. The judge noted, "Let the record show that this is [Ron's] last opportunity." In Ron's case, Jorge underwrote the public defender's plea negotiations with the prosecutor to get a better deal and settle the criminal matter. Judge Edwards, upon learning of Jorge's involvement, overrode the prosecutor's objection and ruled in the defendant's favor by granting Ron another chance at a drug program under Pathways' supervision.

***

The previous chapter brought to the fore that caseworkers and law-trained actors contested, bargained, and co-constructed release criteria. In the San Miguel courtroom community, the daily management of pretrial release petitions reflected differing interpretations of good risks. Release decisions and outcomes were also influenced by institutional pressures to reduce jail overcrowding as well as court officials' increasing interest in referring serious recidivists to court alternative programs. Comparatively, nonprofits scrutinized staffers' power to deny referrals as a means to import greater uniformity and predictability to decision making practices. In this chapter I investigate how caseworkers, in mediation with court officials, orchestrated alternative case outcomes to prosecutorial justice. I primarily focus on the micro level courtroom theater in which caseworkers were cast as legal advocates and assisted in their client's defense. They were not attorneys at law yet they wielded authority with significant persuasiveness over the daily disposition of criminal cases. This chapter specifically explores caseworkers' talking strategies for submitting an oral recommendation to the court including filing motions, brokering pleas, and adding to the record. Analyzing legal talk is a way to understand how court officials and caseworkers attributed meaning to defendants' criminality (Conley and O'Barr 1990; Levi 1990). Defendants' capricious behavior and shaky stories tested caseworkers' ability to finesse legal negotiations. Program staffers in turn rhetorically ascribed alternative meanings to the defendant's delinquency by presenting evidence of the defendant's personal motivation, honesty, and redemption (Albonetti and Hepburn 1996; Bridges and Steen 1998). Staffers' visible presence in courtroom decision making symbolized the expansion of their occupational terrain at the early stages of adjudication yet their bargaining power depended in part on how they were able to position themselves in the court's spatial arrangement. Pretrial release caseworkers were observable courtroom players and much of the legal process was made visible to them. They occupied hallowed spaces of judicial power as evidenced by their omnipresence in the Hall of Justice; they often sat up at the defense attorney's table to present case information to the judge, and they stood at the bench for sidebar conferences with judges and attorneys. In total, I show that caseworkers in the courtroom structured different types of legal encounters between defendants and traditional court professionals.

Filing a Motion

To file a motion, caseworkers submitted a formal application to the court to obtain a favorable ruling for the defendant. There are several general components to filing a motion: caseworkers submitted the necessary legal documents, then orally presented to the court the relevant and supportive facts, and offered up the necessary documents for the judge's signature for purposes of formalizing the recommend course of action. I refer to caseworkers' talking strategies as "pitches" (Emerson 1969, 104), which is an oral recommendation to grant clemency to a defendant. To make a pitch, pretrial release workers talked up the defendant's positive attributes and talked down the negative aspects of the case. In chapter five we read how bail commissioners tested caseworkers' release criteria to negotiate the parameters of a good risk. Caseworkers, as influential voices in the courtroom, successfully reframed criminal matters as worthy of leniency from the court (Goffman 1974), and as such spent significant time preparing cases and thinking through potential problems before they stepped into chambers. Making a pitch was a powerful defense strategy, and oftentimes the defendant's fate rested on the caseworker's scripted courtroom performance.

Second Chance caseworkers presented release petitions to the bail commissioner as part of their routine tasks in the courthouse. On a given day, they screened eight defendants in the county jail and three or four actually "made the cut" as Supervisor Mindy Demarco said, meaning they were recommended release. In a vivid illustration of how pretrial release personnel assumed legal powers to file a motion, Mindy said in reference to caseworkers' discretionary powers to sway the release outcome: "[Presenting cases is] a skill that we have, we decide who gets out and who doesn't." Judicial chambers are traditionally a place where legal decisions are made off the record; the personal and less formal environment allows caseworkers to directly represent the defendant's case. They are hidden from view and inaccessible to the public. Bail commissioners Krupky and Hayes heard cases in chambers every day between 4:30-5:30 in the afternoon or after seven in the evening.[1] Commissioner Krupky's chamber was tucked away in a traffic courtroom on the second floor. Hayes' chamber was situated along a long corridor that runs behind the criminal courtrooms on the first floor. Commissioner Krupky was on duty Wednesday through Saturday and Commissioner Hayes was on duty Sunday through Tuesday. Housed on the fourth floor, Krupky's chambers were white walled; a large institutional pine desk filled the room and was positioned near the window. The desk was neatly stacked with papers, files, and a wilting houseplant. Other than two cushioned chairs facing opposite the desk and several bookshelves lined with legal volumes, the chambers were sparsely furnished.

Case presentations were relatively short; typically two to five minutes yet staff were very much attuned to bail commissioners' particular judging styles and legal orientations and prepared to file the motion for release accordingly. Mindy explained, "With [Bail Commissioner] Krupky, if you have solid information, he's going to let them out. With every judge, there is a way to play it. There's a way to frame it, a way you know they are going to like. With Hayes, he wants to know do they have a place to stay, is someone going to help them get to court." One of the most important features of filing a motion was the skillful pitch of pertinent case information. During my interview with Mindy she humbly noted, "My cases don't have a tendency to get denied that often." The first time I worked in the jail with Staffer Jordan Roberts she gave me her account on the way to present a case. She instructed, "The best way to present to a judge is to quickly say the best thing about the defendant first before the judge gets to the rap sheet." Presenting successful cases provided caseworkers with a measure of their skill and abilities in the courthouse arena and their performance style was a frame of reference for the bail commissioner. Jordan summed up her colleagues' personal presentation styles:

> Mindy is eloquent and will fight to the death; she goes at it. Lawrence [the program director] uses his experience to convince the judge to get someone out and he never gets a denial. Flamine is more serious and presents the facts.

Caseworkers utilized several pitching tactics to win judicial approval of their recommended releases. One method is what I call pitching a plausible story and refers to how caseworkers reconstructed the defendant from an unreliable person to a responsible citizen who can be trusted to return to court. As we read in chapter four, during the jail interview, defendants put forth weak accounts to explain why they did not appear in court such as "I forget." The nature of these accounts denoted laziness, a disregard for the law, poor judgment, or irresponsibility. In chambers, caseworkers retold the defendant's reason for missing court as a plausible story. Mindy explained this rather subtle technique to convince the bail commissioner that the defendant is good risk and of good character. She said:

> [The defendant] says, 'I needed to work.' Instead of saying [to the bail commissioner], 'they didn't want to miss work,' you say, 'He didn't want to lose his job.' If [the defendant] says, 'My mother wasn't feeling well.' You say, [to the bail commissioner] 'His mother was really sick and he had to take care of her.'

As an oral construct, plausible stories reflected caseworkers' "narrative freedom" to construct a compelling explanation for the defendant's noncompliance (Conley and O'Barr 1990, 56). Jordan said, "I need to sell the judge that I think [the defendant] is going to come back [to court]. You can't say 'they forgot,' but it doesn't have to be some outlandish, 'his mother died the day before.' But, it needs to be something." These examples illustrate that caseworkers' success in chambers was dependent upon presenting a case for why the defendant did not appear in court that resonated with the judge's mainstream values of socially acceptable behavior (Emmelman 2003).

A second method that caseworkers used to file a motion was selective omission to prevent a troublesome criminal charge from being raised for discussion. This technique was commonly deployed when the defendant was charged with a serious offense that might reduce the chances of court approval. Jordan explained:

> I don't necessarily bring [the criminal charge] to [the Bail Commissioner's] attention. The [information is] on the booking card; it's just a matter if [the judge] notices. Sometimes you are holding your breath hoping [they] are not going to notice.

Caseworkers' ability to selectively omit information in the defendant's file depended, in part, on which bail commissioner was on duty. Bail Commissioners Hayes's and Krupky's perceptions of risk were partially informed by their occupational experience. For example, if a person had some violence in his or her criminal history, Commissioner Hayes was less likely to approve a release then Commissioner Krupky. This is because Hayes is a former public defender and he had extensive experience perusing criminal justice documents. Krupky, a private defense attorney, was less able to interpret the investigatory file and relied on caseworkers to reveal pertinent information concerning the defendant's criminal history. It is interesting to observe that court officials' relationship to and experience with court technologies shaped their release decisions.

Consider Samuel's case. Just after 6:30 on Monday, I followed Mindy and Flamine Hernandez, another caseworker, as they raced against the clock to get to the Krupky's chambers before his seven pm traffic court calendar to present Samuel's case. Mindy said to me as we took the elevator upstairs, "Sometimes we are running" to chambers. Mindy was worried that Commissioner Krupky would deny the petition for release because of Samuel's criminal record. Nine years ago, Samuel Henderson, a fifty-four-year-old African American man, had pleaded guilty to attempted murder but successfully completed probation and never did prison time. Up until this point since his conviction, he had had no police contacts. He was currently in custody for an outstanding bench warrant for driving with a suspended license. Once Mindy was seated in chambers, Commissioner Krupky quickly leafed through Samuel's paperwork as she narrated the case. She explained that Samuel thought he had cleared his obligation to the court but the warrant was still active. She simply said, "He made a mistake." Commissioner Krupky signed the release without comment. Samuel showed up for court the next morning and the district attorney dismissed the charge. Afterwards, I expressed my surprise to Mindy that the judge approved Samuel's release given this attempted murder conviction. She said, "I know—he (Krupky) probably didn't even see it." Interestingly, Commissioners Hayes and Krupky both stated during an interview with me that they were unwilling to release a defendant with violence in his or her criminal history. The onus, however, was on them to closely examine the defendant's legal documentation. Selective omission as a pitching ploy was successful because judges did not consistently review or read closely the case materials.[2] It is also important to note that caseworkers accurately assessed Samuel as a good risk for release as evidenced by his lawful compliance with the court. If he did not have a caseworker to orally represent his defense, he would have likely languished in jail for the night.

A third pitching tactic that caseworkers used to file motions was offering alternative explanations to suggest that the charges pending against the defendant were less serious than they might appear. An example is provided by Juan Rivera, a forty-five-year-old Latino man. Juan was initially arrested for felony car theft; however, at his court arraignment the district attorney reduced the charge to a misdemeanor: taking a car without the owner's permission. Juan then failed to appear at the subsequent court date and he was rearrested. When Mindy presented Juan's case to Bail Commissioner Krupky, she told of her conversation with Juan's brother, Paul, about the incident. Mindy stated, "I spoke to the brother, and he said the [stolen] car belongs to their cousin, Ricardo." By offering an alternative explanation for the circumstances surrounding the alleged stolen car, Mindy reframed Juan's charge of felony grand theft auto to a possible domestic dispute. Commissioner Krupky nodded his head and signed the release order without comment.

This strategy was particularly useful when caseworkers were presenting hard to pitch charges. According to caseworkers, judges tended to deny petitions with traffic related offenses because they found it irksome that defendants often picked up multiple charges; they were apt to punish the defendant by making him or her spend a night in jail. In an interview, Commissioner Krupky stated with exasperation, "Why can't they just get their license reinstated [before they drive]?" Bail commissioners classified driving with a suspended license as a particularly onerous offense because, in their view, defendants were intentionally breaking the law. Mindy said in reference to the difficulty of getting a defendant out of jail on this charge:

> Defendants charged with suspended licenses end up being the trickiest. The judges get more excited about those than about battery charges. It would be easier to get someone out on [one] battery case than someone who has [multiple] suspended license cases because [bail commissioners] think 'well, [the defendant] just keeps re-offending.'

In the following example, Flamine used the alternative explanation pitch by framing the offender's arrest for a traffic violation in the context of a larger moral imperative (Merry 1990). James Harris, an African American man in his mid thirties, was arrested and charged with driving with a suspended license. In Bail Commissioner Hayes's chambers, Flamine first explained that the Department of Motor Vehicles (DMV) suspended his license for failing to comply with a court order to pay child support. James was working now, she added, to pay back the $1400 in arrears. Flamine then explicitly addressed the circumstances of his arrest to render James a sympathetic character. She pointed out that James was arrested while walking through an intersection. She said, "The police stopped him and ran his name in the computer system." Flamine explained to me after we left chambers that she wanted Judge Hayes to know that James was not once again arrested for driving with a suspended license. The fact that James was on foot, and not driving, might suggest to the judge that James was following the law. Flamine's pitch, however, also broadened the social context of James' arrest, implying that the police may have been operating unfairly, perhaps even with racial discrimination. The bail commissioner signed the release order.

As evident in these ethnographic accounts, bail commissioners were not always privileged with the same level of institutional knowledge and relied heavily on caseworkers' summation of the pertinent facts. In doing so, they were less inclined to rule in opposition to staffers' recommendations. Caseworkers came to expect that the bail commissioners asked similar types of questions about cases and, as we learned in chapter five, they approved the majority of releases. In short, contrary to their prescribed role as legal arbitrators, bail commissioners did not engage in an extensive examination of the defendant's legal documentation; rather, they listened closely to how the caseworker talked about the defendant's case. Bail commissioners however occasionally raised concerns about cases and made an unanticipated ruling. Mindy explained:

> He'll just see something he doesn't like and there's no turning him back. Sometimes it's not even that tangible, it just something he'll see. It doesn't happen that often; He denied people about a week ago. I think the person has a lot of cases and a lot of FTAs or the home situation is not that stable, which is completely dependent on what we have to say.

Caseworkers "filed a counter motion" to convince recalcitrant judges to go along with their recommendations for release and challenged their stated concerns about the defendant's petition for leniency. Counter motions are similar to "accounts" (Scott and Lyman 1968, 46) and "disclaimers" (Hewitt and Stokes 1975, 1), which are linguistic devices used to neutralize negative assumptions and promote legitimate excuses for deviant behavior. One day, in the elevator on the way up to Krupky's chambers, Mindy said to me, "Every once in a while, [bail commissioners] pull a question out of nowhere and I have no idea how to answer." To offset the possibility that the bail commissioner would deny the petition, caseworkers tried to anticipate the potential problems that defendants might represent for the court and entered chambers prepared with a number of other potential pitches to argue for the defendant's release. Staffers employed their discretionary powers to actively contest competing arguments put forth by the bail commissioner about the merits of a case. Mindy displayed her cache of counter pitches for convincing the judge to approve of the release if he is leaning towards a denial:

> I can predict [the] cases [the judge] is going to have problems with and I try to be prepared with arguments. When in doubt, [I] go to 'the jail is really crowded and there's no space for the person' [argument]. Since [our] mission is to reduce jail overcrowding, it is a reasonable approach. If [the judge] is iffy on someone, I will pull that reason out. Sometimes we will get into little philosophical debates. If he has a problem with someone, I'll say 'This person shouldn't be in jail for this, it's ridiculous.'

In common practice, the judge examined the paperwork more closely when they were not entirely convinced by caseworker's oral recommendation to release the defendant. Consider Lenny's case. Lenny Taylor, a forty-one-year-old Caucasian man, was facing charges for vandalism and petty theft. After Caseworker Taj Ramirez presented the information, Commissioner Hayes remained silent as he leafed through the defendant's rap sheet. He furrowed his brow and said, "This guy had a weapons case." Taj talked to me earlier about the possibility that this issue would be raised by the judge and he had readied a response. He explained: "Well, [the case] was ten years ago and it was dismissed [by the district attorney]." Hayes paused to examine the rap sheet again and, seemingly reluctant, approved the release. In the elevator, on our way back down to the jail's processing center, I asked Taj about his success with Lenny's case. He explained, "Part of our job is to advocate. If a case has been dismissed, it's not supposed to be used against [the defendant]." Similar to Emmelman's (2003) study of public defenders' methods for building a case, nonprofit staffers assisted in the defense of their client by putting forth a viable rebuttal to the bail commissioner's suggestion that the defendant was not eligible for release. Bail Commissioner Hayes likely expressed concern about the weapons case because it signaled the defendant's potential for violence. Taj countered that the ten year old charge should not negate the defendant's petition for release; the prosecutor had also dropped the case, which, legally speaking, indicates there was insufficient evidence of criminal wrongdoing. Hayes apparently agreed by signing the release order. In total, caseworkers utilized pitching strategies to portray criminal defendants as low risk candidates for pretrial release, and more often than not, bail commissioners followed their oral recommendations. On par with the public defenders in Emmelman's study (2003), nonprofit staffers assessed the value of a case using the information at their disposal to test the viability of evidence prior to walking into the chambers.

Brokering a Plea

Ron's case in the opening vignette reveals nonprofit caseworkers' involvement in criminal case processing beyond the release decision and their powerfully emergent role in adjudicative practices. Without Jorge's involvement, the public defender would have likely settled Ron's case on the district attorney's terms. While they lacked professional credentials, caseworkers developed credible reputations with traditional courtroom actors which translated into deciding roles in case dispositions. Wayne Brookes pulled me aside at the Open Door agency before I left to shadow Supervisor Lee Mitchell over at the Hall of Justice: "You'll see a different side when you go to court; you see how much juice we have." This is evidenced by nature of their increased responsibility and visibility in the courtroom arena which leveraged their bargaining power. Lee said:

> I think that's one of the benefits [for defendants] of participating in the program is that [we have] a good relationship with the other components of the criminal justice system. Sometimes it does benefit the case. The work that has been done has been good enough that we are viewed as colleagues, as fellow professionals.

John Parks, an Open Door supervisor, provided some institutional history during our interview on how caseworkers cultivated a culture of stability and familiarity among court officials (Eisenstein, Flemming, and Nardulli 1988).

> [When Open Door was first started] the response was positive but many judges had their doubts and we had to prove ourselves by working with judges and showing them we could do the job. We had to prove that our cases were successful, but gradually we were getting more leeway. Early on we were getting 'stupid cases' or 'junk cases.' The system was feeling us out, you know, 'who's this nonprofit in our courts'? With respect to credibility, it hasn't always been this way. It was fostered through hands on with the judges, more handholding and directness with clients.

Caseworkers brokered pleas by negotiating front stage and back stage settlements in order to divert the defendant from criminal prosecution. Diversion typically means that the criminal matter will be dismissed pending the defendant's successful completion of the agreed upon conditions.[3] While pretrial diversion is mandated by legal statute in many states for some misdemeanor offenses, staff successfully negotiated informal diversion agreements.[4] An informal diversion agreement has no legal mandates, rules, or specified eligibility criteria. In the context of this study, it was an agreement between judges and attorneys to allow the defendant to participate in a pretrial release program for a period of three to six months for misdemeanants. As we will read in a later section, the court was also amenable to prosecutorial alternatives for felony offenders through the Open Door, but the district attorney was less likely to dismiss or reduce the criminal charges. To provide some perspective, if the misdemeanant's case was processed through the traditional courts, he or she would likely be sentenced to a few weeks or months in jail. Alternatively, as Caseworker Dave Powell explained to me, "The judges like the program…if [the defendant] can get out on Pathways they are more likely to get a better deal." For example, the defendant may be mandated to attend a substance abuse program, earn a GED[5] certificate, find stable housing, apply for governmental benefits, or obtain mental health counseling. If the defendant complied with the court's order, the charges were usually dismissed or reduced or they received a lesser sentence (no jail time). Caseworkers' involvement in brokering a plea also reduced the defendant's stigma and the emotional toll associated with traditional adjudicative processes. Feeley's central thesis in his book *The Process is the Punishment* (1979) is that defendants in the lower courts experienced lost wages, the inconvenience of multiple court dates and at times poor legal representation. These "pretrial costs" (31) pressured the accused to accept pleas rather than go to trial. Staffers also blamed public defenders' tendency to "put cases over," as Dave put it, as opposed to settling the case quickly. He said:

> I wish some of the [public defenders] treated the clients better. Sometimes they want to keep putting the case over. That frustrates me. I try to push them a little [by asking] 'why are you doing that? What are you looking for?' The PD put over so many of their cases, in my opinion, poor reasons. People have eight or nine court dates sooner or later they are going to bench warrant.

One method that caseworkers used to broker pleas was mediating the judicial process and, in some instances, supplanting the role of the defense attorney by importing their treatment concerns into informal case negotiations. Open Door Supervisor Kelsey Martinez explained her role as a court alternative negotiator:

> We are trying to preempt things. That is what's happening in court. The court representative goes into the judge's chambers and presents the case to the judge and tells them the treatment plan. Then asks the public defender (who might also be in chambers) what they intend to do with the case or where the case is going. The purpose of this is to make sure the treatment plan is geared toward the legal track in order to benefit the client.

Caseworkers' influence over legal outcomes correlates with their access to information and occupation of space and place in the courthouse community. Dave explained, "The capacity that we operate in it depends so much on which courtroom we work in." Chapter two described the problem that some judges were exacting or less amenable to caseworkers' presence in the courtroom. To finesse a courtroom diversion, typically the caseworker and the public defender drafted a settlement and proposed it to the prosecutor. Caseworker Manuela Vega explained, "[Let's say] we have a client that's been arrested for 647(f), that's illegal lodging or camping. The public defender and I will present a plan of ninety days working with [Pathways] and we try to assist him in getting some housing." Manuela cautioned however that the distinct attorney may think the plan is too lenient or inappropriate given the alleged criminal activity. Caseworker Paul Lewis said, in a manner of annoyance, "The [DAs] have this thing set in their mind and all of them do it [ask for six months]. If it's a small case, why not three…or two months, hurry up and resolve it?" Caseworkers' experience dictates that the longer the defendant is on the docket, the more likely he or she will miss a court date, get rearrested, or disappear, which will inevitably derail the plea agreement, which as Feeley (1979) discussed is one of the pretrial costs of continuances. Paul added, "In the cases like that [when the DA objects], we have to step up for the client." "Stepping up" in this context highlights how staffers lawyer against the terms of the plan presented by the prosecutor. Paul explained that the judge often responds favorably to their counter request:

> The judge will pretty much go with our recommendation which is really big respect for our program. The judge can override the DA and his or her opinion and it will stick. That's what we will agree to.

At the early stages of a plea bargain, caseworkers challenged the prosecutorial power of the district attorney [DA]. I observed the following exchange in Judge Michele Davis' courtroom. Allen Jones was a thirty-six-year-old African American man. Homeless for six years, he was arrested for trespassing and petty theft. Mr. Jones stood at the podium alongside Jorge, his Pathways caseworker, and his public defender.

Public defender (*to judge*): Can we refer [for deferred prosecution?]

District Attorney (*to judge*): Mr. Jones [defendant] must do six months [with Pathways].

Judge (*to Jorge*): What is your view? Is that sufficient?

Jorge (*to judge*): No, your honor, I think three months is sufficient.

Judge (*to everyone*): We'll set a disposition next time. Come back and we'll decide on three months.

The significance of this exchange was that the judge petitioned the caseworker's view on the matter to settle a dispute between the attorneys, which provided an opportunity for Jorge to argue against the DA's proposed sentence. Pathways caseworkers reported, and I observed, that judges frequently sought their guidance during criminal proceedings. During an interview, Jorge described his relationship with judges in the courtroom: "The judge will ask, 'Mr. Garza, what do you think we should do? Should we place [the defendant] in a residential [drug rehabilitation] program?' I give my input." Maynard's (1984) theory of the ecology of the courtroom suggests that court hearings are structured by different types of "dominate and subordinate encounters" (243). In this courtroom drama, when the caseworker filed a counter motion, the judge ruled in his favor and the attorneys' customary center stage role receded into the background. Notably, the public defender, although present, did not speak during this courtroom interaction.

In the traditional courtroom, during pretrial proceedings, the judge, the prosecuting attorney, and the defendant's lawyer meet, often off the record, to discuss the defendant's case in an attempt to reach a settlement before trial. Pathways and Open Door caseworkers are often involved in these pretrial conferences in large part because they are the most knowledgeable about the particulars that make up the defendant's criminal, familial, and personal issues. Caseworkers aid in the preparation of the defendant's legal defense by providing information, advice, and investigative legwork to negotiate an informal settlement.

"Our goal is to help the public defender advocate for the client," Kelsey explained. When I shadowed Lee in and out of courtrooms one Friday morning, he said, "We do lot of work [public defenders] simply don't have time for. He recalled a case when his investigative work resulted in earning a dismissal of the charges. In this case, Tim Campbell, the defendant, was facing felony nonviolent charges and he was released to the supervision of the Open Door. As Lee explained it, "[Tim's attorney] didn't know what to do with him. He was a little slow, he couldn't remember much and had head trauma from a car accident. I went to [Tim's] neighborhood to verify the address where the client stayed and talked to the neighbors. I found out that the neighbors take care of him because they know his limitations. I reported this information at a court conference and the DA decided to drop the charges." Of significance, caseworkers made recommendations to the court for how to proceed with criminal matters; they actively culled together evidence to build a tactical defense drawing on their connections with and relationship to community resources.

Open Door caseworkers frequent involvement in preliminary hearings[6] and pretrial conferences[7] in the twelve felony courtrooms led some court officials to mistake them for public defenders. Kelsey recounted a time when she was in Judge Neil Evan's chambers with the district attorney to discuss a case. The district attorney started to ask Kelsey how she proposed handling the criminal manner. Judge Evans halted the discussion and said, "Shouldn't we wait until the public defender shows up?" The district attorney chuckled and said to Kelsey, "Oh yeah, I always forget you're not the attorney." Caseworkers' near universal role in routine court proceedings blurs the jurisdictional boundaries that distinguish them from traditional legal actors which, I suggest, further authorizes them to negotiate favorable deals.

In some instances, caseworkers' familiarity with the courtroom actors empowers them to co-opt the role of the defense attorney and enter into direct negotiations with the prosecutor. Paul described his courtroom role as a stand in for the defense attorney. He said: "I am a mediator between the district attorney and the judge and what's best for the client." Kelsey also pointedly described her attempts to negotiate an alternative to prosecution with the state's attorney:

> Sometimes [we] will ask the district attorney if they know where the case is going to see if the case can be settled. Sometimes [we] can help arrange for a DEJ (deferred entry of judgment) where the client pleads guilty and if they complete their treatment plan the charges are dropped.

As a case in point, I attended a pretrial conference with Kelsey and the attorneys in Judge Richard Kwan's chambers to discuss a case. The defendant was released to the Open Door and he was facing three felony charges related to drug possession. Kelsey told me earlier that she facilitated the public defender's offer to accept the defendant's guilty plea on the condition that two of the three felonies were dropped. Once in chambers, however, Kelsey continued to negotiate for plea leniency by requesting that the prosecutor dismiss the third charge if the defendant successfully completed one year at the Center for Substance Addictions under Open Door's supervision. The prosecutor was in agreement and Judge Kwan sentenced the defendant to earn twelve positive monthly reports from the Open Door on their rehabilitative progress.

Another strategy for broking a plea is courting hallway justice which illustrates how caseworkers pitch for a treatment sentence by capitalizing on the court's willingness to settle a case more quickly by cutting deals. Clara Reyes, a thirty-eight-year-old Caucasian woman, was arrested for breaking a Starbucks' window; she was drunk at the time of her arrest. At the first court date, the district attorney (DA) mandated that Clara attend a six-month outpatient alcohol abuse program. Dave, her caseworker, believed that Clara would be served better by getting housing and counseling for "anger problems." However, Clara failed to appear at the second court date. The court put Clara's case over for two weeks so Dave could look for her. At the third scheduled court date, he did not expect to see Clara, because she had lost contact with the program, but she was sitting in the back row of Judge Theodore Parker's courtroom. Dave spotted the public defender and followed her out into the hallway.

In the hallway, the public defender asked him, "Is Clara going to get a positive report today?" Dave responded, "Clara was doing well [in the program] for two and a half months but she went back to some bad habits. She made it back to court today." Dave pointed out that he was confident he could get Clara "back on track." He proposed settling Clara's case if she earned five months of positive reports, meaning she participate in an agreed-upon treatment plan. Dave told me later that he purposely did not ask whether the prosecutor still mandated Clara to alcohol treatment. The public defender said she did not think the DA would "go for it" because Clara "hadn't done much and she had failed to appear at her last court date" but agreed to present the offer. The public defender reentered the courtroom to talk to the DA and Dave waited in the hallway. A few minutes later, the public defender reemerged into the hallway and ushered Dave into a huddle. She said, "The good news is even though Clara has a spotty record, the DA agreed to dismiss the vandalism charge if Clara stays out of trouble for five months." The public defender warned, "Clara should think of this as a gift and take it seriously. She can't go around breaking windows, enough is enough." Dave and the public defender reentered the courtroom to formalize the agreement with Judge Parker. While he and I waited for the judge to take the bench, Dave whispered to me, "See, no one is talking about drug [treatment] anymore. The thing is people [in court] lose track [of cases]."

Dave argued that Clara should get a second chance at treatment because she returned to court of her own accord, she felt remorseful for disappearing, and expressed motivation to change her behavior. Clara's case further demonstrates that pitching in unconventional venues, such as the courthouse corridor, empowers caseworkers to exploit the law in nontraditional ways. In this example, Dave directed and scripted the public defender's plea offer to the district attorney in the hopes of expediting a settlement for Clara's case that might have otherwise lingered on the docket. The data revealed that public defenders see the defendant's participation in the Pathways program as a part of a possible defense strategy. In total, caseworkers are afforded significant persuasive powers over the daily disposition of criminal cases for misdemeanor and felony defendants.

Adding to the Record

Courtrooms are venues where legal troubles and personal problems become stories that are told and retold (Yngvesson 1989). Feeley describes how defense attorneys attempted to improve their client's record by "manufacturing facts" (1979: 173) or presenting information that would help to produce a positive legal outcome. Caseworkers in the courtroom also contributed to the storytelling process in an important way by providing supplementary information to traditional justice actors to make more informed decisions for how to proceed with criminal manners (Emerson 1969; Feeley 1979; Halliday et al 2009; Nolan 2001). Adding to the record allowed caseworkers to build a case for prosecutorial leniency by positively reporting on the defendant's ongoing treatment compliance. Kelsey explained, "We all know when a client is making progress but we need to be able to show that what we do works to the courts." It is important to observe that the court's increasing amenability to treatment options increases caseworkers' testimonial powers during the early stage of pretrial proceedings. Kelsey said:

> Courts have changed tremendously. The judge wants to know how the
> client is doing. Back in the day, they didn't as long as they show up for
> court. Today, judges are more into treatment for clients than anything.

To add to the record, caseworkers entered into courtroom evidence
oral and written treatment scripts as part of a larger orchestrated effort to
bring about an alternative disposition. Paul surmised the power of this
defense strategy, "[The court] gives [the defendant] credit for just
working with [Pathways] even though there hasn't been a disposition as
far as what [the court] wants [Pathways] to do. [Defendants] actually get
credit for [working with us.]"

One verbal strategy that caseworkers used to enter persuasive
evidence and tap the court's moral accountability occurred during the
court hearings. Adding to the record is a common legal practice in the
courtroom. All formal proceedings are recorded verbatim by the court
reporter to document the legal disposition of cases on the calendar and
seem to be a rather mundane and bureaucratic process. Charlie's case
provides an example of formally adding to the record. It was Tuesday;
Staffer Paul Lewis leafed over a copy of Charlie's status report for
Judge Scott Edwards. Charlie Thomas, his client, sat quietly beside him.
Charlie was a forty-one-year-old Caucasian man, and he had been
homeless on and off for ten years. Minutes later, Judge Edwards took
the bench and called Charlie's case. The public defender, Charlie, and
Paul approached the podium. Significantly, Paul, and not the public
defender, asked the judge, "Have you had a chance to review the
report?" Without comment, Judge Edwards waded through the stacks of
paper on the bench in search of the report. Then he said, "I've found it.
Give me a few minutes." He flung on his glasses and quickly read the
report, looked up at Paul, and prompted in turn, "Would you like to add
anything else for the record?" Paul was responsible in this instance for
Charlie's legal well being and not his attorney because he was more
familiar with the intricacies of Charlie's case. Paul explained that
Charlie could not continue his substance abuse treatment at Willow
Grove, an out-treatment center, due to his medical condition. A car had
hit Charlie five years ago and his leg was crushed. He had had trouble
walking ever since. Paul reported that he was trying to get Charlie into a
residential drug program in neighboring Santa Teresa. Paul then added,
"Charlie continues to comply and work with the program." Judge
Edwards clasped his hands, then rested them on the bench and made eye
contact with Charlie: "Good for you, Charlie. I commend you for your
efforts." The attorneys had not reached a disposition and Paul requested
a thirty day continuance to which the judge and attorneys agreed. Earlier

that day, Paul told me that if Charlie gets into a residential treatment program, it is likely the district attorney will agree to dismiss the charges. Similar to Merry's (1990) study of lower courts, caseworkers draw on different discourses to qualify their therapeutic expertise and to render their client blameless for individual failings. Paul framed Charlie's inability to get into a treatment program as a result of environmental factors beyond his control.

Adding to the court record afforded caseworkers the "narrative freedom" to recount the defendant's efforts to improve his or her life (Conley and O'Barr 1990, 56). In Charlie's case, Paul stressed Charlie's willingness to seek help for his addiction. This empowered the caseworker to publicly document the homeless person's personal, nonlegal plight. Paul emphasized that Charlie's physical ailment limited his participation in the Willow Grove program, rather than a lack of motivation to address his substance abuse problem. Finally, Paul reiterated to the court that Charlie was "compliant" and "working with the program." Paul suggested that Charlie's compliance was evidence of his personal commitment to change because he was putting forth effort. Paul's goal was to convince the judge, as well as the prosecutor, that Charlie's case could be settled in a non-punitive way; it was only a matter of accommodating his personal challenges. This example however illuminates caseworker's dilemma of the "hurry up and wait" approaches to doing justice in the lower courts. Caseworkers requested continuances, as did public defenders, as a strategy to bring about a therapeutic diversion yet these good intentions ultimately prolonged the adjudication of the defendant's case.

In keeping with Nolan's (2001) depiction of the therapeutic theater, Paul's presentation of Charlie's case prompted a compassionate response from Judge Edwards. Nolan writes that common law imposed structural restraints on judges' frame of reference in the courtroom; judges are expected to hold a "passive authority" and behave in an impartial and disinterested manner. As evidenced here, Judge Edwards appeared to be moved by Charlie's plight and spoke directly to him in praise of "his efforts" in trying to get substance abuse treatment. This type of pathos is logged as organizational "credit" towards a possible favorable disposition. In turn, Charlie, the defendant, while typically advised to remain silent during legal procedures for fear of self-incrimination, is also given a voice in the courtroom. Once again, as was evident during these exchanges, the district attorney and the public defender were relegated to the courtroom backdrop.

Barney's case provides another example of adding to the record. It was Tuesday; Dave leafed over a copy of Barney's status report for

Judge Helen Morris. Barney Coleman was a fifty-two-year-old African American man. He had been homeless for twenty-five years and an alcoholic who had been in and out of detox for thirty years. He was most recently arrested for public drunkenness and petty theft. One month after Barney's arrest, the prosecutor still had not decided what to do with the case. Dave hoped he would dismiss the charges if Barney got into a substance abuse program. Barney was recently accepted into Edgewater Drug Treatment program but left after one week. Dave said, "Every time he leaves, he's sorry, he's remorseful." Dave said he is trying to get Barney into another program, "this time outside the city and away from bad influences." But Dave needed time to make arrangements and wanted the judge to continue Barney's case another month.

Judge Morris took the bench and called Barney's case. The public defender, Barney, and Dave approached the podium. Judge Morris briefly reviewed Barney's report and prompted Dave, "Anything you would like to add for the record?" Dave reported to the court that Barney was trying to get into a drug treatment facility. He added, "However, getting Barney stable housing is a priority. He's not inside now." Dave's emphasis on Barney's lack of housing prioritized one set of issues over another; the social problem of meeting Barney's basic human needs had to take precedence over satisfying court requirements. In this instance, adding to the record tapped at the moral accountability of the courtroom.

Dave's mention of Barney's crisis situation prompted Judge Morris to invoke an expression of concern for Barney's plight. After Dave's oral summation, a worried empathy crossed Morris' face. She spoke to Barney directly: "You have no housing, is that correct, Barney?" Barney nodded yes. "Tough situation to be in," continued Judge Morris, "I hope that Dave and his colleagues can be of help to you." Here the judge's words effectively legitimized his homelessness as an important part of the legal disposition. The prosecutor and public defender agreed to continue the case another thirty days. In short, adding to the court record, as a more subtle type of pitching strategy, allowed caseworkers to submit evidence favorable to their client by drawing on the commonplace features of adjudicative courtroom processes. This example also highlights the judge as a compassionate figure as opposed to a disinterested arbiter, which hints at important role changes in the traditional criminal courtroom when justice is outsourced to nonprofit agencies and their staff.

A second evidentiary tactic that caseworkers used to add to the record was scripting a status report before it was presented to the court. Caseworkers submitted individualized reports to the court to provide in depth information on what the client was doing to improve his or her life once out of jail. Jorge explained:

> We will write a status report early on before the decision has been made to put them on diversion or not. We might choose to write a status report just to document we really think this person would be a good candidate [for diversion] because they are already checking in with us regularly and that they've already started these groups, doing this outpatient [treatment], waiting to get into this program. It's a way to let the court know what is going on.

Pathways staffers made a particular effort to hand deliver status reports to judges, prosecutors, and public defenders in order to "see and be seen" as Paul said. Lee of the Open Door echoed this point, "It's important that all the employees do what it takes to maintain that presence in the court...so that we are trusted." On a Tuesday morning, Jorge and I arrived at the courthouse a little after nine with a client, Nicholas Carpenter. Jorge escorted Nicholas to the courtroom and sat him in the back row. Jorge needed to deliver the homeless program's case reports to all the misdemeanor judges, prosecutors, and public defenders. We went to the first courtroom and Jorge asked the clerk if we could go back and hand deliver the report to Judge Nancy Beal. The clerk checked with the judge but she was busy and asked us to wait. The clerk then offered to give the judge the report but Jorge said he would come back later. We then went into Judge Edwards' chambers and he was just ending a conference with some attorneys. Jorge handed him Nicholas Carpenter' status report, which described his participation in outpatient drug treatment and a recent application for SSI. Judge Edwards joked that his was in a large manila envelope. Jorge explained to me later that the judge's copy is more extensive and the attorneys' copy is an abridged version of the report. For caseworkers, making personal visits and joking was all part of assisting in the defense because it fostered collegial relationships with court officials.

Scripting a status report also took place backstage in negotiations with the public defender and at the nonprofit agency. Steve Brown, an Open Door caseworker, explained, "I work a lot with [the public defender] to get this done [a case dismissal]. I made sure that she went to the judge and told the judge the right stuff, the right information to help [the client]." In another example of off stage scripting, Jorge entered the basement office and showed Director Laney Everest the progress report he planned to submit to Judge Morris. She read it over; the status report stated that the client had been going to some groups and he got back on SSI. However, the client had not achieved stable housing. Laney questioned the client's housing situation. Jorge explained: "Well, as far as his living situation, he has been staying with various friends and paying them ten dollars a night." Laney updated the report to read that the client had been maintaining his housing by paying rent, got his SSI reinstated, and was attending groups. Here caseworkers advocated for defendants with transient housing and fractured social ties by expanding the definition of a responsible tenant. Similarly, Steve described how a positive report is produced through an interactional exchange with the client. He said:

> Our job is to give accurate, honest information [to the court] whether it's good, bad, ugly, or indifferent. If I have negative information on a client, I will sit down with the person to see how we can make the shit positive.

Interestingly, Steve played up his neutral role as a court informant but his advocacy role was apparent in his effort to co-script a report that would reflect favorably on the client. Marissa's dilemma was another case in point. Marissa Lopez, a twenty-five-year-old woman, was charged with one count of felony drug possession. Originally, Steve was her assigned caseworker but she was transferred to Tracy King's caseload because she did not want to work with a male staffer. The problem was that Marissa had not shown up for her appointments for several weeks; under Tracy's directive, she was supposed to do a drug treatment program but had not yet followed through. According to Tracy, "the client's mother keeps telling her that she doesn't have to do anything [in relation to the program] and it's confusing the client." At case review, Tracy reported that she told Marissa to make sure she showed up for court the next day. Lee interrupted and asked Tracy what Marissa should tell the court if she showed up. Tracy offered to call the client at home to ask her to bring in some proof of [drug] program enrollment. Mario jumped in and added, "It would be better to tell [the client] to come into the office before court so Tracy can give her referral to Casa De Las Flores [a drug treatment program for women] that she can show to the court. Lee nodded approvingly and then directed Tracy:

> Tell the client to come meet you and Kelsey [at the agency] in the morning and you'll work something out. Offer to bring [Marissa] to the [drug] program right after court. That way, Kelsey can tell all of this to the [judge].

Marissa's case also revealed that another tricky aspect of caseworkers' jobs was negotiating familial interference with clients' contractual obligations to the court and the nonprofit program. These examples of adding to the record illustrate that caseworkers enjoyed a great deal of organizational autonomy over the use and control of defendant information. In particular, they capitalized on their reporting options to influence favorably how court officials adjudicated criminal cases.

Conclusion

This chapter highlighted the ways in which caseworkers' legal maneuvering altered courtroom encounters that governed adjudicative processes. I illustrated that outsourcing justice casts caseworkers as stage managers in a new courtroom drama and that they orchestrated evidentiary tactics to promote judicial clemency for offenders. Caseworkers relied on storytelling to talk about defendants' problems and adopted presentation styles to advocate for clients with a flair for the dramatic and to appeal to court actors' legal orientations. Storytelling in court narrated defendant troubles as "moral tales" (Loseke 2003, 90) and they purposefully foretold of things to come should the judge grant leniency, such as the likelihood that the defendant would return to court or benefit from outpatient drug treatment. Staffers also attempted to package defendants' complex realities into typical legal cases. If caseworkers deemed it advantageous, however, they also de-typified stories by playing up the unusual or unique aspects of individual situations to render sympathy or logical understanding from the court. Pretrial release personnel also learned to finesse the use of talking strategies both within and beyond the boundaries of the courtroom, such as the corridors and private chambers. Caseworkers' success at lawyering however was contingent on the other courthouse actors in terms of who was sitting on the bench and standing at the attorneys' tables.

Nonprofit workers effectively persuaded court officials to adopt jail alternatives which show that nonprofits under state contract extended pretrial release privileges in ways that linked the criminal justice system to local community resources. As a result of these partners in crime, the court's jurisdictional powers expanded to connect defendants to facets of the welfare state because caseworkers and court officials negotiated legal decisions based on the availability of shelters, mental health providers, drug treatment facilities, psychiatric beds at public hospitals, and classes in local educational and trade institutions. This chapter further illustrated that caseworkers redefined the role expectations of judges, prosecutors, and public defenders which effectively disrupted the customary makeup of the courtroom workgroup. At the caseworker's prompting, judges adopt an empathetic authority (Nolan 2001) toward defendants, and they underwrote the public defender's plea negotiations with the prosecutor to get a better deal. Outsourcing judicial decision making to outside providers reorganized the status hierarchies among key courtroom actors and fostered the emergence of normative negotiations for adjudicating criminal matters in alternative ways. As a counterweight however caseworkers' pervasive influence in the traditional legal settings raises the question of whether their "treatment sentences" undermined the adversarial process by co-opting the public defenders' role. One of the apparent consequences of problem solving courts (drug and mental health courts) is the increasing therapeutic control over defendants in ways that gave little attention to defendants' due process rights (Mackinem and Higgins 2007; Nolan 2001) and increased pretrial costs (Feeley 1979). I will explore this issue in further detail in the forthcoming chapter. Policing Compliance investigates how caseworkers supervised clients post release and punished violations with the terms and conditions of the legal agreement. Caseworkers who found clients in contempt of treatment compliance also used the court to leverage their enforcement power.

---

[1] Second Chance caseworkers present cases in between traffic court sessions.

[2] It is possible that the judge did see the attempted murder conviction but because the defendant was sentenced to probation instead of a prison term may have suggested the defendant did not pose a threat to the community.

[3] Pathways caseworkers participate in the criminal proceedings in a decisive manner. For example, the district attorney dismissed the charges against fifteen homeless defendants in the Pathways program upon completion of the treatment plan during the third quarter of 2003.

[4] Diversion can be formal or informal. Formal diversion is a legal statute that allows for eligible misdemeanants to complete a rehabilitee program in exchange for case dismissal. Defendants are who technically not eligible for formal diversion may be able to participant if the judge, prosecutor, or public defender has good cause finding.

[5] General Education Diploma.

[6] The preliminary hearing is an evidentiary hearing at which the state must prove to the judge that there is enough evidence to believe the defendant committed a felony.

[7] A pretrial conference takes place between attorneys to see if the case can be settled without going to trial.

7
Policing Compliance

On a Thursday afternoon, I accompanied Caseworker Steve Brown over to the jail to meet three new clients and bring them back to the Open Door for a program orientation. As we crossed the street, Steve said to me, "The hard part is the clients are so happy to get out and it's hard to get them back to the office." We entered the jail, walked down the main corridor, and approached the correctional officer at the reception window. Steve pressed his clearance badge up against the glass partition and explained he was picking up releases. The deputy nodded assent and slid the necessary paperwork under the divider for his signature which formally released the inmates to Steve's supervision. The women soon emerged through an automated sliding metal door that emitted a vibrating hum as it opened to announce their arrival. They retrieved their property and, giddy with relief at their freedom, nearly skipped down the brightening corridor towards the exit. Steve held up his hands to contain their excitement and ordered them to "hold up and settle down." Once at the agency, Steve directed the women to sit in a small row of chairs close to the doorway. He sat facing them and got right to the point. "You must do the program your caseworker sets up for you. You must come to court and you can be UA'd [drug tested] at anytime. Stay away from where you were arrested. The police will recognize you and be mad that they are out." Steve then met with each woman individually to assign her a caseworker and activate her file in the database.

The next day, Supervisor Lee Mitchell said I should get some practice at "doing releases." He asked me to do an orientation for a new client who he had just brought over from jail. Rodney Trevino, a thirty-nine-year-old African American man, was arrested for drug possession. I instructed him to make all his court dates and check in daily with his assigned caseworker. He interrupted me: "What if I get a job? I'm planning to go into Brighton House [drug rehab center] too." Lee, who must have been listening, approached me and gave me the "timeout" signal with his hands. He pulled me aside and looked in Rodney's file for the release paperwork but couldn't find it. He then whispered to me, "If the client balks [at the conditions], show them the release order [they] signed." Short of holding up the release contract as a prop, he reminded Rodney in an uncompromising tone that he agreed to check in five times a week as a condition of release. Afterwards, Lee said in reference to new releases, "Often clients think the case is ending when in fact it's just beginning."

***

The previous chapter demonstrated how caseworkers draw on rhetorical strategies and fomented productive relationships with judges and public defenders to arbitrate non-prosecutorial outcomes. Staffers' strategic lawyering tactics catered to the nuances of defendants' life circumstances as well as the courthouse personas assigned to criminal matters. All told, traditional court functionaries frequently acquiesced to caseworkers' alternative prescriptions to legally challenging cases. This chapter explores how pretrial release workers enforced the terms and conditions of the defendant's release from jail. Following Bonnie and Monahan (2005), I draw upon the term *contract* to characterize the compliance relationship between the defendant, the pretrial release agency, and the court, in which all parties sign and mutually consent to the conditions disclosed in the document. The offender is legally obligated to attend all subsequent court dates pending adjudication of his or her criminal case.[1] If he or she failed to appear for court or was arrested on additional charges, the client violated the agreement and could be placed back in custody. Historically, defendants released on their own recognizance comply with court demands at a rate comparable to bailed defendants (Thomas 1976). The nonprofits in this study maintained an impressive average failure to appear rate between ten and twelve percent. As we read in chapter five, caseworkers pulled good numbers to build their reputations as risk assessors.

Lee's statement in the opening vignette that the criminal case was "just beginning" alludes to staffers' managerial control over the offender once he or she was released to the pretrial release program. Caseworkers employed various methods to help ensure clients complied with the terms of their release without the cost of a new arrest. Unlike Feeley's (1979) pretrial process model of the lower courts, nonprofit caseworkers, as opposed to the defense attorneys and police officers, were the key sanctioning agents in the courthouse community. While Peyrot (1985) found that counselors claimed allegiance to the client by highlighting their independence from the law enforcement agents, this study supports research findings on problem solving courts that caseworkers realized their quasi-legal status in the criminal courts as beneficial for controlling clientele (Castellano In Press; Nolan 2001). In particular, caseworkers, to varying degrees, used the institutional powers of the justice system and its actors as corrective instruments to sanction noncompliance including program termination. Court officials however failed to abide by caseworkers' requests to discipline violators in part due to their emergent interest in testing the capabilities of nonprofit-run court alternatives. Judges were also reluctant to revoke or remand defendants' release privileges short of them breaking the law. In total, these ethnographic accounts reveal the politics surrounding the definition of legal and therapeutic program compliance as well as courthouse actors' competing jurisdictional powers to enforce the release contract.

Tracking Returns

Second Chance caseworker Samantha Green and I returned from presenting Kevin Vance's release petition to Bail Commissioner Steven Hayes; he signed the order. We returned to the jail and she jangled the keys to open up one of the male tanks and said to Kevin, a forty-five-year-old Caucasian man, "You're going home. Don't fuck up, alright? You have to call tomorrow to let us know that you went to court." The defendant was very drunk and Samantha later said he might not show up although she got a good reference from the residential hotel where he'd been living for three years. Then we went to the main control center to see which deputy was doing releases that afternoon. She approached Lt. David Chan, handed him the signed release form and asked when the inmate could expect to be let go. He replied, "In about fifteen to twenty minutes." One Monday evening, I accompanied Derrick Taylor, a Reach supervisor who worked the swing shift, but he only had one person to release. He did not like doing only one because all the arrestees who were interviewed for OR approached him to ask why they were denied. Cesar Pena, a twenty-nine-year-old Mexican man, was housed upstairs in Pod D. We took the elevator, walked down the white and chrome institutional-looking hallway; the security door began to rattle open as we approached and, once inside, we walked to the command station. Derrick handed the court clerk papers to the deputy; he eyed it briefly and then called for Cesar through the intercom system. He rose from his bunk and we sat at one of the tables in the common area. He did not speak English, so Derrick used his limited Spanish to explain the release conditions which included calling the office in the morning to find out his court date and a stay away order from a local CVS pharmacy. "Tu comprendes?" asked Derrick. Cesar nodded a few times but Derrick was not sure he understood everything because he hesitated to sign his name to the form.

The above vignettes highlight the beginning of caseworkers' contractual relationships with defendants at the point of their release from jail. Kevin and Cesar were not uncommon situations in that failures to appear to court were partially attributable to defendants' misunderstanding about how the court system works. Tracking returns explores staffers' techniques for making sure new clients complied with the basic terms of their release which is to show up to court until the case reaches a disposition. Reach and Second Chance caseworkers provided minimum post release supervision by maintaining phone contact with defendants to remind them of all upcoming court dates. One routine way that the staff tracked returns was making court reminder calls to defendants with an open case. However, this was a burdensome task. Lawrence Austin, the director of Second Chance, explained that making these calls was hard because "sometimes the family and friends get mad because you are calling, especially if they haven't seen the person." One Thursday afternoon, I assisted Mindy Demarco and Flamine Hernandez make calls to defendants two days before their hearing. Each case had at least three numbers to call in hopes of speaking to the defendant or one of the references. Taj Ramirez explained during an interview, "That's why it is important to get phones numbers [during the interview] so we can track them down." I called the first number for Paula; it was her mother's residence. When I asked to speak to Paula Martin, her mother paused with a sigh of exasperation and said "she not here." I asked if she knew how I could reach her and the mother said "no" effectively ending the conversation. I tried the other numbers (one for Paula's best friend and another for her cousin) but both numbers were disconnected. I then rang the first contact number for Charles Schooner; it was also his mother's residence. She answered and was pleasant but she had not seen her son. She explained to me that Charlie actually lived with his brother. When I explained that Charles had an upcoming court date, she added, "[Charlie] doesn't listen to his mother but does listen to his brother." Unfortunately, the brother's phone was also disconnected. The other numbers for Charlie's references were already labeled as "disconnected." These examples echoed common experiences that Reach caseworkers faced in their attempts to remind defendants to appear for court. It further highlights, as we read in chapter four, that defendants and their families often had fragile social connections, and caseworkers had to be creative about how to track down clients once released.

All told, court reminder calls were an effective way to get defendants to show up for court. Since pretrial release agencies shadowed defendants' criminal cases in the backdrop, they were also aware if clients failed to appear. Reach and Second Chance caseworkers however had little leverage to punish or enforce the conditions of the release contract. If the defendant failed to appear in court, the court issued a bench warrant for his or her arrest. When this occurred, another tactic for tracking returns was encouraging the defendant to "add to calendar" before he or she was rearrested. This technique was primarily employed by Second Chance Caseworkers since they had smaller caseloads than Reach. Mindy explained this routine procedure for rescheduling a court date.

> If [defendants] don't show up, then we contact them right away and say, 'you need to get back on calendar.' If they don't show up for court, it automatically becomes [another] bench warrant. The police have priorities so they are not going to send a SWAT team. Most of the time they can [add to calendar] before they are rearrested.

Adding to the calendar involved going to the county courthouse and standing in line at the court clerk's office. It was however often a long, arduous, and bureaucratic process particularly for someone of limited means. The staff tried to reach the person on three occasions, but if the defendant did not make contact with program or add to calendar, they placed the names of program violators on what they called "the shit list." Taj explained, "If they don't follow through after a while then we put them on our 'shit list' so the next time they come to jail we wouldn't get them out anymore. We only get hit once." Once the person was on the list, they were not eligible for release through the program for three years.

By comparison, the Pathways and Open Door programs tracked returns using intensive community-based supervision techniques. Defendants were mandated to meet with their caseworkers at the office or to phone in up to five times a week. Caseworker Paul Lewis said, "With mentally ill clients especially we need to keep a tight rein on them." Once the defendant was out of jail, caseworkers talked about the stressful demands of spending inordinate amounts of time finding clients who failed to show up for court or simply disappeared. One strategy that Open Door caseworkers employed for tracking down defendants who missed court was called a "lost and found." As we read in chapter one,

William Rand, a forty-six year-old-African American man, was released to the supervision of the Open Door but he never came back to the office. Kelsey initiated a "lost and found" which meant that caseworkers looked for him at his routine hang out spots near Seventy-seventh and Peachtree in the Northside area of town. Similarly Paul said that sometimes he will be driving down the street and see a client who has not checked in for a while. He said, "It's happened two or three times. I pull over and try to talk to the person. A lot of times people are ashamed that they didn't follow through on the program or that they're in trouble." To reduce the enormous amount of time and energy looking for lost clients, caseworkers tracked returns by luring clients to the office for food, a shower and a place to use the phone. They also used the incentive of a hotel room if homeless clients continued to abide by the program rules. Paul said, "We try to motivate clients to do better." When Pathways "lost" clients they were placed on what caseworkers called, "the hot list" which meant finding them was a high priority. Casey (his street name), for example, was on the hot list because he had not been checking in with his caseworker, Manuela Vega, who was soon scheduled to escort him to the neighboring county courthouse to appear on another criminal case. In another example, John Marlin, a forty-four-year-old Caucasian man, was released to Pathways and Jorge, his caseworker, put him up in a residential downtown hotel for a week. Now John was on the hot list because he failed to appear in court. At the staff meeting, Jorge explained that John was a recycler which meant he was often around town picking up cans and bottles and redeeming his collections for small sums of money. Jorge hoped to find John near the can and bottle redemption center before he got picked up on a warrant.

Staying the bench warrant was also part of caseworkers' toolkit for remedying the challenges they faced tracking down missing clients. To stay the warrant, the caseworker asked the court to suspend the police arrest until they had an opportunity to locate the person. Paul explained that his decision to "ask for a stay" hinged on his relative certainty that he could get the client back to court. He said:

> It depends on how good my contact is with that person. If that person has come in every day or three times a week, I will try to get the court to stay the bench warrant for a week or so. In one situation, the case got called and the public defender went up and I stood up with her. She explained what was going on, talked a little bit about why client wasn't there and we would like to stay the warrant. The judge asked to hear from me. I explained why I thought that we could get him into court a week from that day. I was in touch with the father, the client is there every morning, and he told his father that he didn't have court. I

have this really solid contact and I'm confident that we'll be able to work something out. In other cases, the DA might object to staying a warrant but they don't that often.

It is important to observe that the nonprofits differed in terms of their level of community-based supervision with the defendant post release. The pretrial release conditions for the Open Door and Pathways programs crossed over into what I call a treatment contract. In addition, to attending court hearings, caseworkers required defendants to submit to random drug testing; obtain stable housing; and participate in group therapy, substance abuse treatment, mental health counseling, or employment training. To keep clients engaged in long term treatment was challenging and the staff members learned to anticipate that clients would drop out of the program or fail at treatment several times. Caseworkers developed graduated forms of leverage to gain willful consent from defendants to which I now turn.

Requesting a Bench Lecture

In the previous chapter, caseworkers advocated for judicial leniency by pitching the defendant's positive attributes. Conversely, to request a bench lecture, caseworkers offered information to the court in grievance of the defendant's disobedience, what Emerson calls a "denunciation" (1969, 104). They effectively used the court as a platform to reproof defendant's failure to abide by the terms of the release. Open Door and Pathways caseworkers' access to chambers allowed them to initiate a bench lecture before the court proceedings began.[2] Open Door staffer Victor Smith explained how bench lectures amounted to caseworkers' directing, nay puppeteering, the judge's front stage performance in the courtroom:

> [A lecture] means that they are not messing up bad enough to get revoked, so [we] want the judge to give them a stern warning from the bench. It's a weird ventriloquism because the judges have no idea what's going on. We just say lecture them and the judge says ok.

Each morning, Kelsey Martinez and Lee made the rounds at twelve felony courtrooms picking up referrals, delivering progress reports, and requesting lectures for defendants who did not check in or failed to follow through on required programming, such as attending alcoholics anonymous meetings. Kelsey explained to me, "When it's court time, the [caseworkers] look at the progress assessment and reports. If the defendant hasn't been checking in or following through [on the program] then the court knows about it." Caseworker Steve Brown explained the conditions under which he requested a bench lecture to compel a defendant to adhere to the conditions of his or her release. He said:

> I can ask the judge to kind of shake him up. Sometimes the client [is] coming in and checking in but they are doing nothing. I get [them] three referrals [to social services] and every time he loses it. 'Give this man a lecture. I'm not going to remand you this time; I'll give you a lecture. Get your mind right.

Importantly, a lecture is warranted if the defendant breached the terms of the "treatment contract" although he or she was in compliance with the legal terms of the release by maintaining contact with the agency and attending court hearings. Mileski (1971) identified verbal reminders or reprimands issued by judges to defendants in the courtroom as four types of situational sanctions: good natured, bureaucratic, firm, and harsh (523). Correspondingly, the data revealed two basic types of bench lectures: encouragements and reprimands. *Encouragements* involved asking the judge to motivate the defendant to comply with the terms of the release. To meet the particular challenges of working with homeless offenders, Jorge Garza explained how this technique was useful for managing troublesome clients:

> We do communicate with judges a lot, particularly if we want them to sort of manipulate what's going on. If we have a client that we are really trying to encourage them to get into treatment and he is stalling a little bit. If it's coming straight from a judge, the client will listen a lot of the time. Technically, they [clients] are under no obligation to us to do anything. The treatment plan that they work out with us is a condition of their release but it's entirely voluntary. We can't issue a bench warrant if they don't show up at our office. We have no power in that respect. Determining how to keep a client motivated or encourage them to follow through is tricky, so we try to use the court to our advantage to some extent.

To augment their authority, staffers tapped the court's power as a means to persuade clients to participate in their treatment plans. Jorge justified his authority by saying "We are up to speed on where the client is and what they are doing. Lawyers don't know what is going on with their clients. We have done a lot of work to earn credibility." Consider Lily's case. Lily Morgan, a twenty-two-year-old Caucasian woman, was facing charges of vandalism and public drunkenness; she was released from jail into the Pathways program. Lily, however, failed to appear for two subsequent court dates. Jorge, her caseworker, asked the judge to stay the bench warrant and made a number of attempts to contact her on the street. On the morning of Lily's next court date, Jorge searched the courtroom hoping she would show up. He was relieved to see Lily sitting in the last row of Judge Judith Fenton's courtroom, looking somber and whispering to her new friend, Frank. Frank and Lily had first met moments earlier on the courthouse steps. Lily introduced Jorge to Frank and explained his presence: "I was scared to come up here alone." Jorge reassured her, "There's no reason to be scared and I'm really glad to see you." Lily flashed a nervous smile and crumpled the hem of her shirt.

Jorge headed back toward Judge Fenton's chambers. She was donning her black robe, readying herself for the day's calendar; he knocked gently on the doorjamb and she ushered him in. "Lily's here, she came to court," Jorge informed her. He then asked the judge to "remind Lily that she can't miss any more court dates." Judge Fenton happily agreed. Shortly thereafter, Judge Fenton took the bench and called Lily's case. She rose from the back bench and Jorge escorted her to the podium to stand next to the public defender. The judge smiled and said, "Good morning, Lily. We missed you last week! Jorge assured me that you would come back to court. It's good to see you. It's very important you continue to do well and come to court." Lily, looking wide-eyed, nodded in agreement. In a whisper, Jorge prompted her to say, "yes, Judge" for the record and she readily complied.

In Judge Fenton's courtroom, defendant noncompliance did not warrant what Melossi (1990) calls "reactive social control," (149) such as the direct threat of punishment. Rather, the judge, in collaboration with Jorge, persuaded the defendant to adopt normative standards of behavior. The front stage (Goffman 1959) of the conversational exchange between Judge Fenton and Lily appeared to reinforce the traditional structure of the courtroom: the judge is the legal arbiter and sanctioning agent. Yet Judge Fenton's remarks to Lily were underwritten by Jorge's back stage solicitation in chambers. In chambers, Jorge solicits Fenton's assistance in garnering Lily's compliance and requested that the judge remind Lily of her obligation to the court. In the courtroom, the judge, prompted by the caseworker, issued a hopeful message to the defendant. For example, the judge said (somewhat tongue in cheek) that "we" (the court) "missed" Lily, as opposed to admonishing her for failing to appear and temporarily disappearing from the program. This is similar to the therapeutic culture of problem solving courts in which the judge and team members address the client's failure to make progress by building up their self esteem (Castellano In Press). In closing, Judge Fenton encouraged Lily to "continue to do well," which was a reference to her earlier progress. In issuing a bench lecture, caseworkers' treatment goals benefit from the judge's ability to encourage defendant compliance by issuing a few well-chosen words from the bench. It is important to emphasize that the judge would not issue a bench lecture, at least not in this fashion, without the prompting of the caseworker.

In another example of an "encouragement lecture," I accompanied Kelsey to Judge Janice Lee's courtroom. As we crossed the street, Kelsey explained to me: "Our agency advises judges on what we want them to do with our clients." We entered the Hall and walked straight back into Judge Lee's chambers to talk about a "problem client." Dave Holliday was a forty-year-old Caucasian man charged with felony drug possession. Mario ordered Dave to participation in drug addiction counseling as a condition of his release. However, he had yet to show up to any of the weekly meetings. Kelsey explained to Judge Lee that "[Mr. Holliday] is resistant to substance treatment and is still using." She requested that the judge "encourage [the defendant] to attend the treatment sessions." The judge nodded in agreement and added that she would call this case first. It was common practice for the judge to deal with caseworkers' clients first so they did not have to wait as the court waded through a heavy docket. In this sense, caseworkers reduced the pretrial costs for defendants related to criminal case processing. In the courtroom, the judge took the bench and told the lawyers she would call Mr. Holliday's case first since "Ms. [Kelsey] Martinez" was present in the courtroom. The defendant rose and stood at the podium flanked by Kelsey and his public defender.

> Judge Lee (to defendant): Mr. Holliday, it's hard to make changes, isn't it?
>
> Mr. Holliday (to judge): [He nodded 'yes.']
>
> Judge Lee (to defendant): It's very important that you try. Do you know what the Riverside [drug treatment program] is?
>
> Mr. Holliday (to judge): No.
>
> Judge Lee (to defendant): Well, I'm sure Ms. Martinez can explain it to you.

At Kelsey's request, the judge continued the case for two weeks. The practice of requesting a lecture illuminates caseworkers' considerable influence behind the scenes to encourage treatment compliance. Afterwards, Kelsey revealed to me that she thought that the client feigned ignorance of the drug program in anticipation that the judge would sanction him. As discussed in chapter four, caseworkers had misgivings about defendants' true commitment to recovery. Holliday's situation illustrates that caseworkers further accused defendants of manipulating circumstances to their own ends. The use of the "encouragement lecture" reveals that judges heeded to caseworker's requests because they were also invested in a court alternative outcome. Interestingly, in both examples, the judge framed the caseworker as a helper or counselor when in actuality they were the key sanctioning agent behind the lecture. This helped the caseworker to achieve the treatment goals while reducing the risk of alienating the client.

The second type of bench lecture was a reprimand and involved asking the judge to orally censure a defendant in the open courtroom based on the caseworker's reported account of program noncompliance. At the Open Door, Otis Stewart's case was set for a judicial reprimand. He was a thirty-five-year-old Caucasian man charged with drug selling and released to the Open Door. On the Tuesday morning prior to the scheduled court hearing, Mario met with Otis to inquire why he had not been checking in. Otis replied, "My lawyer said I didn't have to check in." After Otis left, Lee, who had overheard the exchange, kidded that he would like to ask the court to have both the defense attorney and Otis remanded into custody. Mario agreed, "Yeah, I got [Otis] out. He's on *my* caseload." Otis challenged his oversight authority by claiming that his privately retained attorney's legal counsel superseded the program rules. On Wednesday morning, I accompanied Lee to the courthouse; we went straight to Judge Herbert Mills' chambers to update him on several clients. Lee reported that Otis had still not checked in with his caseworker, Mario. Several weeks previously, he had put in a request for a bench lecture to address the same problem. Lee reported to Judge Mills that Otis had not contacted the agency since the first lecture claiming his private attorney told him he was not obligated to check in. The judge looked at his calendar and said the defendant was being considered for a felony diversion program. Lee explained that until Otis was officially accepted into the program, he fell under the supervision of the Open Door. Minutes later, Judge Mills took the bench and court was called to order. He called Otis' case first since Lee was present. Otis' attorney stood to address the court and requested a six week continuance. Judge Mills called the attorney and the prosecutor forward for a sidebar discussion. When they approached the bench, the judge asked, "So you want a six week continuance?" The attorney explained that his client was provisionally accepted to the diversion program. Then the judge called on Lee, who sat at the public defender's table, to address the matter. Lee stood up and said, "Your Honor, [Otis] was released to the Open Door and there was some confusion with regard to his obligation to check in. His lawyer told him he did not have to check in." Judge Mills held up the signed release order by the corner which ordered the client to report to his caseworker five times a week. He admonished the client and his lawyer citing Otis' obligation to continue to check in with Open Door because he "was released on that condition." The lawyer stood with his hands clasped in front and defended Otis' actions: "Your Honor, my client works at UPS and will be starting a full time job training program." The judge asked the attorneys "is a modified check-in [with Open Door] is in order" but then he looked to Lee for a recommendation. Lee responded, "He could check in by phone once a week." "Pick a day," said the judge to Lee. He replied: "Wednesday." The judge then turned his attention back to Otis and gave him a stern warning: "It's not asking a lot to call in once a week. It's easy to find a pay phone, or get to a phone, a cell phone. If it's reported that you haven't been checking in, I will put you back in jail." The parties were dismissed and Lee was pleased that the client and his attorney were staunchly reprimanded by the judge.

These examples illustrate several points worth highlighting. First, bench lectures leveraged compliance by threatening the defendant's program standing including the possibility of a jail sanction. Second, the judge reinforced the caseworker's law enforcement authority in the courtroom by referring to Lee as being on par with the attorneys and requesting that Lee rather the defendant's lawyer modify the check in conditions. Third, Eisenstein, Flemming, and Nardulli's (1988) research illustrated that the stability of courtroom workgroups bred familiarity among members and thus shaped criminal case dispositions. Here Otis' private attorney, as an outsider, was less aware of the courthouse culture that granted caseworkers' discretionary powers to set and modify the terms of compliance. Interestingly, Lee blamed the attorney's lack of understanding or even arrogance regarding his client's legal obligation to report to the Open Door for the "confusion" that ensued. In these examples, the caseworker's backstage role was to co-script the judge's front stage role in the courtroom. This method of policing compliance essentially enhanced the judge's informational power in the courtroom which, in turn, increased the court's social control over the defendant. Caseworkers are the central persons that come into contact with defendants once they are released from jail. Accordingly, legal officials granted caseworkers a great deal of autonomy to manage their caseloads, which offers further evidence of the power they hold in the Halls of Justice.

Revoking Releases

Caseworkers terminated program services for clients who repeatedly failed to abide by the conditions of their release which is similar to probation officers who recommended repealing an offender's suspended sentence. There was an interesting distinction between revoking and remanding as mechanisms of social control. To remand refers to placing a client back into custody. At the program orientation for three new clients, for example, Mario Alvarez issued a warning: "Stay out of trouble, [If not] I'll put you back in jail or rather you'll put yourself back in jail." In practice, Kelsey explained, "We try to not to do that [jail remands] too often but sometimes it does happen." Caseworkers had no formal capacity to re-incarcerate people but they retained the power to issue revocations if deemed necessary. Steve explained, "Revoked means we want [the client] off the caseload. We have too many clients to waste time with someone who's not trying to follow the program." The program can terminate program services but, as Kelsey explained, "It is up to the courts to decide what to do with the defendant."

The research on drug treatment courts has found that judges routinely use jail sanctions, also called motivational jail or flash incarceration, to punish clients for failing to conform to the behavioral expectations of the program (Burns and Peyrot 2008; Hora, Schema, and Rosenthal 1999; Nolan 2001). In traditional courts, however, caseworkers had difficulty revoking or remanding releases because the court was generally reluctant to drop persons from the program or re-incarcerate them once they were out of custody. Dave Powell of Pathways explained:

> Judges don't like throwing people back in jail. If they are out, they don't bring people back in. I've only had a couple of clients remanded over my time and just being out of custody makes the court view you so differently. I don't think judges would like to hear that but it's a reality. If you're out of custody, putting you back in custody is clearly a big deal. It's just not something the court does that much.

When a person is discharged from the program for noncompliance, the court usually allows him or her to remain at liberty pending a case settlement. This is because caseworkers often drop clients for failing to complete treatment, which the court may not view as a violation worthy of returning the offender to jail. Reach caseworkers experienced a similar problem of judicial noncompliance when they reported that defendants were not abiding by the court-mandated check ins. Rafik said, "There are a few judges that take the supervision very seriously, but many don't." Rafik said, "Nothing ever happens. There's no punishment. The punishment is the judge says stop doing that, start calling in more. But, I've never seen anybody remanded. If they're already out, it seems like too much work [to put them back in jail]." Judges were particularly reluctant to jail or drop clients who caseworkers accused of "treatment offense" as opposed to a legal violation. My field notes revealed that judges raised concerns about caseworkers' power to revoke clients from the program. Judges, as well as public defenders, noted that the decision to terminate should be reserved for persons who violated the legal conditions of their release, such as being rearrested and charged with additional crimes. Caseworkers, however, found cause to drop clients if they did not commit to treatment. This expression of differences suggests a disparity between program staffers and court officials with regard to the fundamental purpose of pretrial release services. Judge Theodore Parker who presided in the felony courts, stated to me during an interview:

> [Pretrial release programs] were never about [defendants] doing a program. The purpose is to make sure the person comes back to court. [These programs] provide that intense supervision. Some of the programming sounds like fluff.

In some instances, when a defendant failed to abide by caseworkers' therapeutic mandates, judges suspended formal law in favor of a less punitive response to a defendant's recalcitrance. Caseworkers in turn sought to revoke noncompliant clients by dropping them from their caseloads without legal intervention because judges failed to enforce program requirements.

Orchestrating a Judicial Bypass

To orchestrate a judicial bypass, caseworkers subverted the court's authority in order to terminate clients from the program. Consider Travis' case. Travis Perkins, a thirty-nine-year-old Caucasian man, was diagnosed with a serious mental disorder. He was ordered to complete counseling, take medication, and live at a residential housing facility for persons with mental illnesses. However, he had been a difficult client for some time; he physically threatened Mario, his caseworker. When he failed to show up in court, Kelsey requested that the court issue a bench warrant for his arrest and remand him back into custody. In spite of her recommendation, Judge Lee wanted "to talk to the client," as Kelsey put it. She stayed the warrant and gave the client one week to show up in court. Kelsey explained that Judge Lee's ruling was "a setback" because the client still resided in one of the agency's residential hotel rooms.[3] Mario recalled that "The client never should have been at hotel in the first place," but the client's public defender asked Judge Lee to place him there and Kelsey was obligated to provide him with housing. Kelsey, in consultation with her staff, decided that Travis posed too much of a danger to staff and other clients; on the basis of his mental instability and propensity to be violent, the staff justified evicting Travis from the hotel. Kelsey noted that if "they take away the client's housing" it will compel the court to place Travis back into custody. She said, "If there's trouble [getting Travis out of the hotel], the guard should call the police and have him arrested."[4] In this example, caseworkers manufactured conditions to force the court to re-incarcerate Travis. The staff anticipated the court would follow suit because he posed too much of a public safety risk if he was homeless and on the streets without supervision. Orchestrating a bypass was a tricky strategy for caseworkers to carry out in part because the court was less willing to jail persons short of committing another offense. To achieve this policing strategy, staffers subversively regulated the actions of judges and attorneys as well as the recalcitrant client.

Another example of a judicial bypass in a more subtle form occurred on a Monday afternoon during case review. The Open Door staff gathered to discuss the status of active cases. Matthew Curtis, a twenty-nine-year-old Caucasian man arrested for possession of heroin, was released to their supervision the day before. The client was reluctantly accepted by Lee as a personal favor to Judge Neil Evans who wanted Matthew to go to drug treatment. Lee said, "I hope he fails and I expect him to. He'll fail to show up at the substance abuse program and he'll be off our caseload." While Lee yielded to Judge Evans' legal authority to release the client into the program, he also planned to cite the program rules as grounds to terminate him for therapeutic noncompliance. The Curtis case shows the conditions under which treatment mandates superseded the lawful conditions of the OR release.

Another tactic that caseworkers used to orchestrate a judicial bypass was purposefully opting out of opportunities to advocate for clients, including letting a warrant issue against a client. As we read earlier, caseworkers had the power to request that the judge stay the warrant to avoid a new arrest. At times however staffers purposefully elected to let the bench warrant issue. The warrant and subsequent arrest were a remedy for dropping clients from the caseload. Jorge said of John Marlin's (the recycler) case discussed earlier in the chapter: "If he isn't found and he gets picked back up on the warrant, we might drop him from the program. We usually do." The larger strategy was explained by Paul Lewis:

> We don't always want to stay a bench warrant. For our program, we actually request that the bench warrant not be stayed. We only want to do it when we are really certain we can get someone back [to court]. The public defender is more ready to stay a bench warrant because they don't want their clients to warrant. If someone has disappeared, we don't want the warrant to be stayed that day because we have no way of knowing if we'll be able to find them for a court date the following week. In that case, we'll say a bench warrant should be issued.

Caseworkers also qualified their authority by purposefully failing to appear during courtroom hearing as a means to opt out of legal negotiations. Generally, Pathways caseworkers are philosophically opposed to keeping defendants in jail for such things as arrests for minor crimes or drug relapses. However, there are times when staffers terminated clients by physically avoiding the courtroom at important decision-making junctures, what I call "withholding testimony." For caseworkers, dropping out of legal negotiations was necessary because homeless defendants who repeatedly engaged in deviant behavior (e.g. get rearrested or fail to show up for court) may jeopardize the program's reputation. In an interview, Jorge talked about Gene Holt, a thirty-three-year-old Caucasian man, facing charges of loitering and assault. He explained:

> Gene was not doing well. I told the public defender that I was not going to be able to advocate for [him]. [Pathways] let Gene out [of jail] twice before. It would make us look bad by advocating and have him do poorly again. If he's going to get released on his own recognizance, I don't want to interfere with that. I'm not here to try to keep him in jail. I'm not going to advocate against him. We try to avoid the courtroom. I'll tell the public defender [I can't advocate] but then I will not go into the courtroom.

By withholding testimony, caseworkers divested themselves from the courtroom negotiations. When the caseworker is not present in the courtroom, he or she forces workgroup members to adopt a legal course of action without their informed opinion: keep the defendant in custody or release the defendant on his or her own recognizance. If released, the defendant cannot be referred back to Pathways without the expressed consent of the caseworker, which further absolves staffers of responsibility for the defendant's actions. Jorge gave a vivid account of revoking clients in progress. He was trying to avoid being asked to comment on Marshall O'Connor, a fifty-two-year-old Caucasian man, who was back in custody on a new charge. He recalled:

> I was in the courtroom [for another case] but I tried to sit off to the side. The public defender requested OR [for Marshall]. The district attorney knew [Marshall] was working with [Pathways] and asked me to say something. I went up slowly, [the court] kept talking. The judge agreed to OR so I didn't have to say anything. If [the DA] made me say something, I would have said '[Marshall] is not doing so well right now. I'll continue to work with him, but I don't think I can advocate to get him out right now.'

As apparent in Marshall's case, staffers can withhold information that might be useful to the court, which, in turn, passively asserts control over the court's decision on criminal matters. Jorge explained: "if [the client] has been working with me and I've advocated against [re-releasing the client], they'll keep him in. My negative comment is definitely going to make them [court officials] say 'forget it' [meaning hold client in custody]." The above examples highlight that staffers' jail-sanctioning powers can also override the efforts of the defense attorney to deflect or minimize the court sanction. In a comparable approach, Kelsey and Lee of the Open Door responded to client noncompliance by "Letting the court handle it," which meant not advocating for or against the client at the next court date. The examples of *letting the warrant issue* and *withholding testimony* are on par with Nolan's (2001) finding that treatment counselors play a prominent role in the drug court theater in that they are empowered to keep back information during the weekly status hearings.

All told, caseworkers experienced some difficulty revoking clients from their caseload and remanding recalcitrant offenders into custody because judges opted to keep them engaged in treatment. Their punitive powers were tempered by judges who became committed to helping offenders meet their rehabilitative potential. As we have seen, however, judges may advocate for treating clients that caseworkers would just as soon remand back into custody. Lee of the Open Door noted this trend among judges. He said, "The client's case is a yardstick. The judge is trying to test the program to see what caseworkers can do with difficult clients at the extremes." This chapter also illustrates that caseworkers have also effectively expanded the depth and breadth of their oversight powers. The shift was apparent when judges compared pretrial release programs to probation. During an interview, Bail Commissioner Hayes describes probation officers as "desk jockeys" and caseworkers as having a "hands-on approach." Kelsey explained to me why judges prefer pretrial release over probation: "The court knows that probation is hard to work with, [Reach] only does call in supervision; Open Door is a catchall because we have credibility in court." Furthermore, caseworkers and judges have different orientations regarding the nature as well as the scope of pretrial release services. Theoretically, they have different institutional parameters for defining a "criminal defendant" in compliance with the law and a "good client" in compliance with treatment. The court required that the defendant attend all subsequent hearings pending adjudication of the criminal matters and desist from any further police contacts. Comparatively, a good client obligates the offender to pursue treatment and recovery services, make counseling appointments, and demonstrate a willingness to better his or her life. In total, the agencies ability to enforce the rehabilitative mandates shows that they developed their own internal rules of compliance for defendants that run parallel to and in contrast with the rule of law.

Conclusion

One of the primary responsibilities of pretrial release programs is helping to ensure defendants are present in court and tracking down those who fail to appear. This chapter explored caseworkers' methods for monitoring compliance and sanctioning noncompliance. Caseworkers used jail-alternative strategies to leverage both clients' conformity to the rules and orchestrate a punitive response to program violations. Along with finding "lost clients" as a means to hold legal sanctions at bay, caseworkers also induced judges to encourage, reprimand, and revoke justice-involved persons who did not abide by the programmatic terms of their release. To staffers' chagrin, however, court officials laid claim to their jurisdictional authority to suspend punishment in the interest of treatment. It is interesting that caseworkers adopted law enforcement terminology, such "remanding back into custody" and "revoking programs services" to describe their managerial powers. Throughout the book, staffers' evolving supervisorial roles influenced not only the when client's pretrial release case began but also when it ended.

This chapter also raises the spectre of coercive compliance when justice is outsourced to nonprofit agencies. Once released to the supervision of pretrial release programs, defendants are subjected to forms of discipline that may have little to do with the adjudication of their criminal case. In becoming a client, the defendant is subjected to the supervisorial mandates of private agencies. Jose's following statement points to a key concern among critical criminologists that intensive supervision programs widen the net of social control over marginalized populations, many of whom would most likely have their charges reduced or dismissed in the formal legal arena (Caputo 2004; Nolan 2001). [5] Jose Marino, an Open Door client said to Mario, his caseworker, during a rather tense check in session, "I do have to be here because the courts ordered me here. If I don't come, I'll go to jail. I have no choice." Outsourcing justice casts the net of social control over larger numbers of low level offenders with "smaller holes" which makes it more difficult for individuals to disentangle themselves from the justice system. Under government contract, the pretrial release programs in this study theoretically contribute to the expansion of the court's jurisdictional powers over offenders. In Ibarra's study (2005) on an electronic monitoring program, the participants are defendants who have not yet been convicted of any crime as opposed to probationers who are sentenced to complete certain terms. Similarly, my study supports the finding that the intensive surveillance provided by pretrial release programs at the early stages of adjudication allows the courts to increase its powers over people who have not yet been convicted.

The empirical chapters revealed that nonprofits operating in the judicial system under government contract redefined conventional expectations of courthouse community members. Chapters five, six, and seven showed that judges demonstrated an emergent treatment authority to offer jail alternatives to recidivists. Chapters four and seven in particular illuminated that defendants turned nonprofit clients are expected to show motivation to change their lives by participating in agency-regulated and court-monitored treatment plans. In chapters six and seven, court officials deferred to caseworkers' recommended courses of actions. Throughout the book, nonprofit caseworkers expanded their judging, lawyering, and policing powers to make decisive decisions regarding the direction of criminal cases at the pretrial stage. I now turn to the concluding chapter to show how privatizing justice brings about a new pretrial career for law trained actors, outsourced agents, and the criminally accused.

---

[1] As discussed in chapter two, the release conditions may also stipulate a stay away order from the place or persons associated with the pending criminal charge.

[2] There were occasions when the judge called Reach staffers into the courtroom to speak about the poor compliance history of a defendant but Rafik said, "Generally we don't make court appearances."

[3] The agency was granted state funds to purchase a block of hotel rooms for offenders with serious mental disorders.

[4] One caseworker expressed concern that if Travis went back to jail under non-compliant conditions, he would be prosecuted under the Three Strikes Law.

[5] An alternative view is that alternative jail programs are not coercive but rather they provide defendants what Bonnie and Monahan call an "expanded choice" (2005). Defendants' participation in pretrial release programs is not coercive to the extent that they are made aware that they have the option to go to court and request a bail reduction or release on his or her own recognizance through their defense attorney (see Bonnie and Monahan 2005).

8

New Courthouse Careers

Pathways caseworker Paul Lewis and I entered Judge Helen Morris' courtroom. He told me that Eddy Brent, a client, was "graduating" today, which meant his misdemeanor charges of illegal camping and petty theft would be dismissed. We sat in the first row of the court's audience section, immediately behind the public defender's table. We had to wait a little while but soon Colleen O'Rourke, Eddy's public defender, called his case. Paul took the podium and motioned Eddy to stand at his right side. Paul gave a summary of his achievements. "He's done very well in the program. He's been going to AA meetings regularly, he's moving into transitional housing, and plans to go to the Community Health Center for continued drug abuse treatment." Judge Morris expressed her enthusiasm and congratulated him: "I'm proud of you," she said. The public defender moved for a formal dismissal of the charges and the prosecutor agreed. Paul patted Eddy on the back and escorted him out into the hall. Eddy smiled widely and shook his head "I can't believe it," he said. The public defender came out of the door soon after and shook hands with both of them. "It's a pleasure to work with you," she remarked to Paul. Paul then made plans to accompany Eddy to "an instant hearing next Tuesday" to take care of an infraction charge for an open container so he could finish up his criminal cases.

***

Eddy's graduation day exemplifies caseworkers' expansive role in the criminal justice process from the point of referral to legal disposition. Without Pathways' involvement Eddy would not likely find leniency from the court. He was ineligible for pretrial trial diversion and facing a jail sentence due to extensive police contacts and prior convictions. Short of posting bond, his chronic history of court noncompliance meant that he would in all probability remain detained pending the outcome of his case. The matter was adjudicated by a different kind of court organization in which outsourced agents mediate traditional adjudicative practices. The dismissal of the criminal charges was largely orchestrated by Paul's lawyering for an informal diversion agreement and hinged on court officials' willingness to sentence Eddy to community-based treatment. The court ultimately vacated the charges since Eddy complied with the conditions of the negotiated plea under Paul's supervision.

This book reflects a larger theoretical project about the phenomenon of what I call outsourcing justice, which considers the institutional impacts of contracting out judicial decision making to nongovernmental agencies. Judges delegated their authority to outside caseworkers to help them make informed decisions about which defendants are entitled to release without bond. Nonprofits however broadened the scope and depth of their participation in criminal court proceedings to the point that they occupy a nearly universal role in the justice system. This point is represented by Open Door Supervisor John Parks when he said to me in an informal interview, "We drive the system to function around us. We're in a unique position." John's statement not only denotes the centrality of caseworkers' tasks in the criminal justice system but their ability to dictate with relative autonomy how the courts function. In total, the book's findings revealed that privatizing aspects of judicial decision making to contracted agents redefines the parameters and practices that shape traditional legal processes well beyond the decision to grant OR release.

The notion of outsourcing justice speaks to larger debates on contemporary trends in crime control and punishment. Many scholars are writing about the demise of the rehabilitative era that aimed to correct or fix offenders and the shift towards instituting actuarial instruments to assess, predict, and minimize offender risks (Garland 2001; Feeley and Simon 1992).[1] Some probation departments for example employ standardized risk and need-based assessment tools, such as the LSI (Level of Service Inventory), to calculate the probability that a person will reoffend if released into the community. The function and task of advocacy-oriented nonprofits in the criminal justice system however hints at a resurgence of the old penological model. Court officials, in partnership with contract caseworkers, endeavor to achieve individualized justice for defendants by appropriating punishment based on the unique circumstances of each criminal case (Dixon 1995; Savelsberg 1992; Ulmer and Kramer 1996). Fox (2005) suggests that the distinction between rehabilitation and risk respectively is a false dichotomy particularly since offender rehabilitation and its formative ideals are still present in many corrections based programs. Certainly the adoption of pretrial release programs and their expanded capacities is evidence of a recommitment to reformative over punitive responses to crime, similar to how Nolan explains the emergence of drug court as "the pathological shift" (2001, 133). Nonprofits convey substantive judging criteria to discern individual risk to public safety as well as their potential for community-based supervision in ways that level equal access to the law. Granting outside providers the largely discretionary power to influence if not dictate an inherently legal decision constitutes a social policy to divert the costs of incarceration to community-based programs. These micro and macro linkages speak to the ubiquitous power of the culture of law as it operates through daily decision making practices both inside and beyond the criminal courtroom. As a cautionary note however outsourcing justice to nongovernment agents means that the administration of justice is meted out to the accused by persons other than law trained actors. Nonprofits, as organizational actors, embrace their task to move legal cases to different institutional outcomes but they are also inspired to import the values of restorative justice into the halls of justice. I return then to the foremost question posed in the book about what happens to routine justice when justice is for hire.

Caseworkers' pervasive role in the criminal justice system is best supported by the evidence that court officials are making different decisions because they are following the recommendations of contracted agents. Nonprofits were successful in their endeavor to change the way business is done in the criminal courts as evidenced by the fact that they are now commissioned to carry out judging, lawyering, and policing functions. As illustrated in the empirical chapters, caseworkers were empowered to evaluate the worth of pretrial release referrals and, using available resources, cull together evidence that will be viewed favorably by court officials. They were also able to reject referrals they deemed ineligible or untreatable. At the local theater of the courtroom they frequently took on lawyerly activities to assist in offenders' legal defense and sanction their level of noncompliance. To transport alternative justice claims into formal courtroom settings, caseworkers employed a range of material, rhetorical, and symbolic resources to influence a judicial determination. Chapters four, five, and six illuminated that caseworkers' evaluative powers were enhanced given that they had a great deal of access to personal and technical data to compile cases that traditional court functionaries needed to make lawful determinations. They knew defendants' files and records better than court actors: they interviewed arrestees, summarized their criminal history, talked to their families, and verified their housing situation. Caseworkers also held discursive power to make a pitch for releasing petitioners and framed offenders' legal problems in ways that resonated with court officials' sense of rehabilitative justice. Staffers frequently emphasized that charisma and good speaking skills were just as important as assembling the necessary paperwork (Biggart 1989; Weber 1968). On par with defense attorneys, caseworkers took on the task of casting reasonable doubt in the court of law. As we read in chapter six, they assessed the "viability of evidence" to discern the potential to persuasively reconstruct events in such a way as to counter the prosecutor's rendition of the facts (Emmelman 2003, 43). Caseworkers also relied upon the symbolic nature of the courtroom drama by narrating the defendant's sympathetic characteristics to the audience in the hopes of garnering judicial clemency.

The book also brings to bear that nongovernmental actors are necessarily better equipped to make more inclusive decisions that more fairly weigh criteria to assess criminal risk. While all four nonprofits operate with the best intentions to provide helping services, staff persons had their own cultural, moral, and legal ideas about which defendants were legally entitled and socially deserving of nonfinancial release. Release on one's own recognizance is a promise to abide by all conditions imposed by the court in lieu of monetary bond. The criteria for evaluating a person's ability to keep that promise invited a range of factors that potentially led the purpose and intent of the law astray. Chapter four revealed that in many ways caseworkers repurposed the definitions of classic risk factors such as community ties to grant homeless persons the benefit of OR release. They also embodied systemic practices and cultural assumptions about the notion of privilege that reproduced inequalities, including subtle forms of racial and gender coding as we read about in chapter five. Alternative organizations like Reach, Second Chance, Pathways, and the Open Door are founded on the ideals of individualism, democracy, and social justice. Theoretically speaking, members aim to break down traditional hierarchies to find common goals through acceptance of differences. In these unconventional environs, rules and procedures are replaced by processing members' feelings and emotions (Kleinman 1996). This alternative approach to casework was apparent in chapter four when staffers screened potential clients by "making a hook" with the person to solicit their story and then "listening beyond" for evidence that the defendant was ready to make a change in their lives.

In Kleinman's book *Opposing Ambitions* (1996) she found that bureaucratic elements still persisted, including status hierarchies and the emergence of protocols for structuring organizational activities. They were hidden or less visible because they manifested in different ways which undermined the organizational mission of the alternative health organization. Chapter five showed that perceived biases were called openly into question within the agencies and caseworkers held each accountable for making more open-minded decisions. Interestingly, court officials also, in effect, broke down barriers and "keyed open the iron cage" by challenging caseworkers' judging criteria to increase the number of defendants released under community supervision. Moving social justice values into criminal courtrooms also meant that nonprofits unintentionally exacted new pretrial costs. Foucault (1979) predicted that less oppressive mechanisms (e.g. electronic bracelets and random drug tests) would devolve out of formal correctional practices. Chapter seven detailed that ways in which nonprofits and their employees were authorized to act as a powerful cadre of both therapeutic and legal control. Operating with the authority of the courts, caseworkers used their influence to dictate the terms and conditions of pretrial release decisions.

In total, nonprofit staffers poised on the boundaries of the criminal justice and social justice worlds were involved in judging pretrial release referrals, lawyering for alternative justice, and policing defendant compliance. Throughout the book I showed how defendants and court officials also took part in newly assigned roles, which were accompanied by shifting responsibilities as well as differing approaches to standard adjudicative processes. I conclude that outsourcing pretrial release decision making to private agencies maps out new courthouse careers for the primary agents and the criminally accused.

New Pretrial Careers

In one of Blumberg's (1967b) classic works, he represented a machine model of court organizations in which criminal cases are managed by a set of law trained actors in a bureaucratic fashion in order to meet production norms. In this vein, courts are people processing organizations in the manner that Hasenfeld (1972) wrote about. They function to filter cases through to various institutional outcomes[2], and individuals who pass through are granted a new public status (i.e. defendant, convict, probationer, and inmate). An offender's "court career" begins when the police officer makes the arrest and the prosecutor files formal charges to seek a conviction. The accused is finally betrayed by the defense attorney who uses duplicitous tactics to induce a guilty plea (Blumberg 1967a).[3]

As we read in the introduction, courts in practice are not bureaucratic organizations in the classic Weberian sense. Weber (1968) theorized that societies would be characterized by increasing rationalization of modern bureaucracies that traps individuals in efficient technical systems and the accomplishment of organizational goals takes precedence over the welfare of individuals and the impersonal rationality is prized as a basis for making decisions. Conversely, as we have seen, organizational actors in the courthouse community are participating in what Flemming Nardulli, and Eisenstein (1992) call a "professional setting and a political arena" (10). In these surroundings, legal decisions are governed by a shared interest in releasing defendants from jail safely and judiciously resolving criminal matters. Contract caseworkers and traditional court functionaries also negotiate decisions with a vested interest in advancing personal and professional goals. Drawing on Goffman's (1959) notion of the "moral career of a mental patient" and Blumberg's (1967a) idea of the "moral career of the accused," I draw a parallel to an arrestee's court career through the pretrial release agencies. Nonprofit caseworkers are the principal agents which begin once the person is court referred to the program for evaluation.[4] Following Paik (2009), I use the term institutional career because the defendant's fate is determined by law enforcement and social service workers as well as their sponsoring organizations. Outside providers are involved in its primary phases: the risk assessment stage, the case bargaining stage, and the compliance reporting stage. Caseworkers, in their agent capacity, are responsible for promoting, demoting, and terminating defendants' pretrial careers from the point of arrest to adjudication. Judges and court officials, as secondary representatives, facilitate career beginnings and aid in law and treatment related decisions by deferring to staffers' recommendations. In all, outsourcing justice casts caseworkers, court officials, and defendants in new courthouse careers. Specifically, caseworkers are cast as court alternative specialists, court officials as treatment facilitators, and defendants as criminal justice clients.

Caseworkers as Alternative Court Specialists

Outsourcing basic judicial processes opens up the possibility for alternative justice ideals to affect systemic reform. The occupational aspirations of contract caseworkers are to make the law accessible to underprivileged persons who are frequently subjugated by class stratifications in the criminal justice system. Chapter three illuminated that caseworkers' up-and-coming careers as court alternative specialists were tempered by their lack of professionally recognized credentials. Consequently, part of their larger task was building reputable skills and gaining recognized competence short of having papers to legitimate their influential authority. Some paraprofessionals are becoming "professionalized" as new government mandates require certification or some formal demonstration of competency to work in public institutions, such as schools. Likewise, national and state pretrial release associations established best practices and organizational guidelines to increase the professionalization of its workforce.[5] Caseworkers, in learning to walk the fine lines between alternative and conventional approaches to justice, adopted strategies to reconcile tensions between these opposing ideals. This was not without compromise or consequence. One of the dilemmas of becoming professionalized was that extending program privileges to defendants was bound up with the agency's reputation for quantifying low failure to appear rates. Caseworkers had to prioritize their own career reputations by rejecting referrals and dropping clients who failed to meet expectations. For example, Reach caseworker Anthony Banks said he reminds defendants that when they do not show up for court, "they not only ruin it for themselves but also put the program at risk." For caseworkers, taking on policing functions was another sacrifice of their values and not an easy career transition. Lawrence Austin of Second Chance asked me to fax a warrant for one of their clients who did not show up for court. He explained that, in part, he was disappointed in the person for "flaking out," but even worse was acting as an adjunct to the sheriff's office, an uncomfortable reversal of roles. Caseworkers' jobs placed them in the position of exercising law enforcement powers which undoubtedly undermined their commitment to jail alternatives.

This notion of a new courthouse career for treatment professionals in the criminal justice system holds promise for investigating other alterative courts that are similarly staffed by outside social service providers. The adoption of problem solving courts has increased the level of involvement as well as the visibility of treatment providers in criminal courtrooms (Castellano in press; Nolan 2001). Notably, many mental health court case managers in my study mirrored the occupational backgrounds of the contract pretrial release caseworkers. Most held college degrees not all were specially trained or licensed in behavioral health or substance abuse. Very few had prior experience working with criminal justice populations. Like the pretrial release workers in this study, in addition to the primary tasks of supervising the client in the community, they took part in tasks officially regulated by specialized training including procuring evidence of client noncompliance, drug testing, and property searches. This begs the question of whether contract social service personnel would be making different decisions if they were regulated by a government or educational entity. Does their occupational autonomy give them a greater ability to make progressive decisions and act outside of the proverbial box? We have to be careful to assume that professionals without papers in governmental positions of power necessarily results in aberrant outcomes or unequal decision making practices. All organizational actors have to make decisions about problems taking into account taxed institutional resources and politically charged environments. Certainly nonprofits under state contract have competing sets of constituents and they have to strategically respond to a variety of demands and, in the process, make difficult choices about who benefits from their services and why. Importantly, this book shows that contract social service providers have demonstrated, short of formal credentials, that they are adept at recognizing possible contingencies to client problems, compiling fractured pieces of information and responding creatively to complex situations.

Nonprofits also advanced their careers by further institutionalizing their programs to both fiscally secure their position and expand their services into other legal areas. Caseworkers saw themselves in competition with other criminal justice departments, including Adult probation and the Office of the Public Defender to develop better, more efficient, more responsive methods for resolving criminal matters. In this vein, they keyed law enforcement occupational arenas to advance their careers. Their success was facilitated by judges in particular. During my interview with Bail Commissioner Steven Hayes, he described his decision to refer a defendant to supervised pretrial release instead of probation as "a no-brainer." The court's decision to shift away from probation as a monitoring agency effectively translated into enhanced career opportunities for contract caseworkers. In one of the Midwest mental health courts I studied the probation officers were not even members of the treatment team. The treatment manager explained their absence as "it was redundant," meaning that case managers acted in dual capacities as treatment counselors and correctional agents (Castellano In Press). During my research tenure, the Pathways program expanded its services to include intensive home detention case management to individuals who had violated the terms of their probation and were facing revocation. Open Door and Pathways were also involved in a two year state-funded pilot program to assist offenders with severe mental illness.[6] As suggested in Wayne's opening vignette in chapter three, caseworkers sought out growth opportunities during periods of fiscal crisis and budget reductions. Lawrence anticipated that the capacity of his program would grow after the sheriff announced that one of the off-site jails would be shut down as a cost saving measure. In all, these new initiatives demonstrate pretrial release agencies' opportunistic nature to expand their range of services as well as the makeshift nature of criminal justice policy making (Jacobs 1990).

Law Trained Actors as Treatment Facilitators

The basic roles and responsibilities of courtroom judges are to follow legal procedures, make a legal ruling on guilt or innocence, pass down sanctions, and rule on motions (Feeley 1979). Judges under common law for example are obligated to abide by statutory law and rule in a fair, impartial manner, what Glendon (1994) calls "interpretative and personal restraints" (118) respectively. Interestingly, as we have read, court officials' legal authority manifested in innovative ways when decision making was outsourced to contract caseworkers. Judges negotiated on the job training with caseworkers acting as counsel and rendered legal decisions that departed from the parameters of formal legal procedure (Nolan 2001). This is evidenced by the company they kept in the nonprofit's organizational domain; they visited the agencies to learn about treatment options, to dropped off referrals, and to inquire about the direction of criminal cases; and they called staff persons on the phone to personally pitch referrals. Judges' investment in rehabilitating chronic offenders contributed towards redefining justice ideals in the courthouse community in ways that facilitated treatment-based sentencing options in traditional courts. The court officials in this study expressed confidence in and fondness for the nonprofits and their staff because they believed that they helped defendants to be responsible and accountable to the system. They looked to these programs to help address defendants' social, medical, or psychological problems and, consequently, over the years, law trained actors adopted a much greater restorative approach to criminal law as a consequence of working closely with caseworkers and their respective programs. In short, they often took on the informal role of treatment facilitators rather than legal arbiters.

Judges also launched new careers in problem solving courts, and a recently published *Judge's Guide to Mental Health Jargon*[7] suggests career assistance for those involved in specialty dockets. Judges participate in these new legal forums because they are opportunities to take a different approach to crime problems. Judges, under what Nolan (2001) defines as "un-common law" (90), are able to respond more flexibly to noncompliance and negotiate the particulars of individual cases. They have greater access to community resources. In my mental health court study, following the advice of treatment providers, judges wrote letters on behalf of clients, for example, to employers and apartment owners to help them secure employment and housing respectively. Nolan (2001) reported that drug court judges find their role in the specialist docket more satisfying because they are making a difference in a person's life.[8] In the opening vignette, Judge Morris expressed enthusiasm for Eddy's successful completion of the case. Judges' willingness to facilitate alternative court outcomes was further evidenced in how they articulated their relationships with program staffers. Judge Will Hwang said to me during an interview, "Social work is really necessary. I think it's a waste to time...to jail the population, you can't do it. Jails can be part of the solution...We have to redefine what we define [as] success." This helps us to understand that court officials' willingness to defer to caseworkers stems from an acknowledgment that prosecutorial and correctional approaches to adjudicating cases are not always appropriate for chronic offenders.

As we read in the empirical chapters, one of major outcomes of outsourced justice was that caseworkers advanced to the front stage of the courtroom and attorneys receded into the backdrop. Recent studies have found that attorneys play a minimal or downplayed role in these alternative court settings, so much so that one of the informants in James Nolan's book (2001) referred to the drug court prosecutor as a "potted plant" (82). In my current research on specialty dockets I found that some programs are not staffed by attorneys at all. This reveals that as treatment courts evolve, legal professionals are not only less visible actors; they are no longer even in the courtroom which suggests an occupational demotion of sorts. There are clear implications of court officials adopting treatment facilitator roles in terms of defendants' due process rights. Judges' level of enthusiasm for helping offenders to become productive citizens masks the defendant's contractual obligations to abide by court-mandated treatment without a criminal conviction in many cases. The judges and attorneys in this study also referred defendants to pretrial release programs to thwart the adversarial process and test the capacities of programs to handle difficult referrals all of which prolonged the case settlement. Judges also made personal appeals to the programs to take on, what caseworkers called "pet cases" which suggests that court officials are advocating for some individuals and not others. All told, judges' foray into the treatment world holds promise for "reinventing justice" (Nolan 2001) but there should be avid debate regarding the court's capacity to rehabilitate justice involved persons in balance with the procedural protections of the law.

Defendants Turned Nonprofit Clients

The defendant's ability to advance his or her pretrial career from jail to the community was determined at the crossroads of criminal justice and nonprofit worlds. On the one hand, nonprofits' commitment to restorative justice expanded the possibilities for pretrial release as well as informal diversion for the most challenging offender populations. On the other hand, once released, the defendant fell under the purview of both the criminal courts as well as the nonprofit agency. At the forefront, the defendant's career potential hinged on caseworkers' constructions of his or her legal and private troubles as amenable for community-based supervision. We read in chapter four that caseworkers judged court-referred defendants as good risks if they were forthcoming and willing to work on their self. Upon release, the defendant turned client was subjected to caseworkers' imposed mandates to check in regularly, participate in substance abuse treatment, find employment, and sign up for public benefits. In total, these types of client-centered activities are associated with rehabilitating the defendant's troubled self and they are distinct from the procedural processes in the courtroom (Gubrium and Holstein 2001). Program staffers use their sanctioning powers to establish and enforce the contractual conditions under which defendants are released from jail, which could arrest their pretrial release career if they failed to comply. Criminal offenders are then burdened with managing dual statuses: a *defendant* of the criminal justice system and a *client* of the nonprofit. The construct of the criminal justice client raises the issue of whether they are fully and knowingly consenting to the terms of their release (Redlich 2005). To hold a client status denotes that the person is accepting services voluntarily and participating in decision making to some extent. As we saw in chapter seven, some arrestees were released when they were drunk and therefore mentally incapacitated or they did not speak English. Both instances, at least theoretically, precluded their ability to sign forms with informed consent. What degree of autonomy, if any, do clients have to negotiate the terms of their involvement in the program? Defendants at times challenged caseworkers' oversight authority such as the example with Otis Stewart in chapter seven who claimed that his private attorney's counsel superseded Open Door's check-in rules. The judge sided with Lee Mitchell, the caseworker, by threatening to put him back in jail. In my view, the "voluntariness" of these dual statuses is problematic. A more accurate depiction of the defendant's participatory role in pretrial release services is coerced voluntarism (Peyrot 1985 and also see Burns and Peyrot 2003). When given the option to remain incarcerated or get out jail, however, most arrestees opt for the latter and concede to the conditions with little power to protest.

Defendants' potential for a promising career was further complicated by the fact that some caseworkers also held prior criminal convictions. This was not uncommon. Nolan (2001) found that drug court treatment providers were also recovering drug users and Joel Best (1999) writes that counselors are often "professional exs, individuals with little formal training...who have began careers helping others in recovery" (124). At least one-third of nonprofit employees reflected the population of the clientele, primarily African American and Latino from poor or working class backgrounds with little or no college education. They grew up in the same communities as many of the criminal defendants, had spent time in jail or prison themselves, or had justice-involved family members. Open Door Caseworker Steve Brown voiced how his own past criminal career enabled him to relate better to defendants in the county jail: "I've been there. It's different for me. When I come up on the sixth floor and walk down that tier, there are a lot of faces in there that I know. They jump out their bed, 'man, if you change your life around, there's hope for me.' Man, that's huge." Others were harsher judges of character because they had experienced similar life hardships and successfully reinvented themselves into productive citizens. Tracy King stated, "I've been where they are so I feel comfortable telling them off." Peer counselors in treatment-based programs are effective components for aiding clients' transition into recovery, but how these persons translate their experiences into a helping profession is an important issue for consideration.

The defendant's new courthouse career is further evident when we consider the structure and function of problem solving courts. Once accepted, clients are required to attend weekly court review hearings to report on their progress toward recovery. Similar to Eddy Brent, persons graduate from the court program once the team members determined that they had regained mental stability, desisted from criminal activity, and demonstrated an ability to live independently. The court's routine operations are structured by a system of rewards and sanctions to encourage treatment compliance as well as hold offenders legally accountable for their actions. There are few studies that have examined the contexts surrounding the role of offenders turned clients in this new court organization. My study on mental health courts suggest that clients enjoy a more autonomous role because they are encouraged to take ownership of their own career by showing initiative and gaining independence. The local culture of these programs also empowers clients to bear witness to their recovery by rhetorically drawing upon the therapeutic ideals of the mental health court which, as I have documented, they use to earn credit for compliance and escape punishment for wrongdoing. Further research is warranted to understand how offenders justify and explain their recalcitrant behavior as well as the conditions under which they challenge the court's authority.

Conclusion

I conclude that outsourcing basic case management responsibilities to private sector organizations reengineers the administration of justice and sets defendants, caseworkers, and court officials on a new pretrial career course. The book lends credence to a therapeutic turn in criminal justice institutions which suggests the limits of legal authority in addressing the fundamental causes of crime in society. Court officials are open to collaborating with nongovernmental agents to solve a host of institutional problems. The book showed that outsourcing justice involves actors moving restorative justice values into the corridors of courthouse. As part of this structural shift, jail overcrowding and court recidivism are culturally defined as symptomatic of individual pathologies and societal inequalities. Nonprofits are hired as state created entities to help provide court involved persons with greater equality before the law and connections to helping services in the community. It must be acknowledged that these agencies are charged with tackling some of the most intractable social problems that law trained officials encounter, such as homelessness, drug addiction, and domestic violence and do so with little funding or public visibility. Along the topography of the contested terrain, these agencies have found creative ways to bridge institutional differences with their partner in crime and have shown that bureaucratic methods and standards can serve as tools for advancing alternative agendas.

At the heart of the book, I address the question of whether contractual governance encumbers and unburdens the democratic ideals of equal justice in a free society. The nonprofits in this study reduced the burdensome pretrial costs levied against defendants by doing investigatory and defense work to broker alternatives to incarceration. While caseworkers wanted to make progressive criminal justice decisions to assist primarily poor defendants, they also had limited staffing resources and strong ideological views on which individuals they were willing to accept onto their already burgeoning caseloads, which suggest a potential shadow side of their involvement. All told, the work of these nonprofits has illuminated, in many ways, that they can effectively balance advocacy for legal change and government accountability for fiscal solvency which emboldens their great potential for transformative justice in the criminal courts.

---

[1] This is commonly referred to as the difference between the old penology versus the new penology.

[2] This is what Blumberg (1967b) refers to as the "sieve effect" (50).

[3] The defense attorney's legal relationship to the defendant is tantamount to a confidence game and the client is the mark (Blumberg 1967a).

[4] It should be noted that nonprofit pretrial release programs also act as way stations before the defendant passes on or transfers to other institutional careers, including jail and prison, probation, or other diversionary court programs.

[5] The source for this datum is California Association for Pretrial Services' Releases Standards and Recommended Procedures http://www.pretrialservicesc a.org/docs/CAPS_Standards_022807.pdf (Accessed September 2nd, 2010).

[6] After the first year, the monies for the program were eliminated due to state wide budget cuts.

[7] The reference was accessed on November 17, 2010. http://www.prainc.com/xml/services/popups/judges_guide.html

[8] My study of mental health courts reveals that judges use rhetorical strategies to gain willful compliance from justice-involved offenders, including metaphorical discourses to encourage struggling offenders and prosecutorial tactics to test their commitment to the program.

Appendix
Pretrial Career of an Ethnographer

This appendix details my own pretrial career as an ethnographic researcher in the San Miguel County Courthouse. I will describe my courthouse career in terms of how I forayed into the field site as well as my roles and responsibilities at each pretrial release agency. I then discuss some of the dilemmas that I faced and how I managed them in the contexts of the field setting. The reader should note that some of this material was previously published in the *Journal of Contemporary Ethnography* (Castellano 2007).

Career Beginnings

I began my field research at the San Miguel criminal courts with prior experience working in a correctional institution. I taught literacy at a state prison facility and I was also involved with an organization that provided support services for visiting families of prisoners. These programs were operated by nonprofits that were committed to improving the lives of offenders once they integrated back into free society. Prisons, depending on their level of security, accommodate outside community groups to the extent that they serve an institutional need and do not obstruct the primary mission of security. I explored the possibility of carrying out a research project on the role of nonprofits in prisoner rehabilitation. However, the logistics of gaining approval from the Department of Corrections was not methodologically feasible at the time.

An acquaintance who knew of my research interests introduced me to a contact person affiliated with pretrial release services at the San Miguel county jail. I completed field research at Second Chance and Pathways in 1998 and 1999. I expanded the study to include Open Door and Reach in 2002 and 2003. I returned to conduct follow up research in 2003 and 2004. I found that, in comparison with the prison, nongovernmental workers in criminal justice systems have greater degrees of freedom to advocate for change. The caseworkers in this study believed that their participation in the local courts was the best opportunity for shifting crime control policies to alternative interventions. Open Door supervisor Kelsey Martinez declared assuredly during my caseworker training: "Anything is possible with the courts." Pathways director Laney Everest expressed the urgency of diverting defendants from traditional prosecutorial justice. She said to me during an informal conversation: "Once people get on that bus [to prison], we've lost them." I found that the caseworkers wanted to tell their story. I was afforded generous access to these research sites and I came to know the people in the organizations quite well.

My level of involvement at each pretrial release program varied depending on what I was able to arrange with the directors. At Second Chance, I observed caseworkers interviewing defendants and presenting cases in chambers. I helped to prepare cases, verify references and make court reminder calls. I also provided project assistance to the director on compiling quarterly and monthly reports. At the Pathways program, I spent time in the office attending staff meetings when caseworkers reviewed all the active cases, reported on what happened in court, and discussed new referrals. I sat in on client counseling sessions. I spent the majority of my time however shadowing caseworkers when they took clients to court. At the Open Door, I was an unpaid caseworker for twenty hours a week and carried out all or most of the same duties assigned to line staff. I had a small caseload of ten clients; I usually had to do one or two jail interviews a day and also had to attend case review and present my court recommendations to the group. I also spent time working as a staff person at the Reach program. I spent fifteen hours per week observing and conducting jail interviews, making court reminder calls, picking up police reports, checking in clients and dropping off cases to the bail commissioner. Aside from my scheduled fieldwork at each program, I also made an effort to be present at different times of day. I volunteered to come in early, work late, and work on weekends. I also attended special events; for example, I accompanied Reach caseworkers to Judge Will Hwang's swearing in ceremony and I attended Open Door's annual Christmas party.

Career Training

I spent many hours in the county jail learning how to read booking cards, do interviews, and update case files using the court management system. There were times when operations were quiet and cells were less populated, yet the ebb and flow of arrests is inextricably linked to protests, police raids, demonstrations, and even the disbursement schedule of welfare checks. The people who worked for pretrial release agencies are knowledgeable and dedicated but their jobs involved direct service with an emotionally taxing clientele. The county jail housed persons with severe and untreated mental illnesses and substance abuse problems. It was difficult to conduct interviews when the inmate was in drug withdrawal which was euphuistically referred to as "dope sick." Reach staffer Rafik Nara explained, "Sometimes you have to be aware of the nature of the place; It's jail. Some [inmates] are extremely angry and sometimes they curse you out a few times before they realize that you're there to help them out. Yeah, they think I'm a cop and they tell me 'fuck off, fuck you motherfucker, I don't want to talk to you.'" According to caseworkers, you had to be "thick-skinned" to do their jobs.

I observed many interviews before I started doing my own. I also completed caseworker training sessions at each of the nonprofit agencies. Second Chance and Reach also gave me copies of extensive employee manuals to reference. At the Open Door, Kelsey asked me and other trainees to participate in "mock interviewing." Lee Mitchell played the role of the defendant and slipped into the characters of an angry and mentally ill person with impressive ease. On the second day of the training, we did "mock check ins" to learn how to ensure clients are complying with the conditions of their release. Kelsey advised:

> Take control of the call but give options to the client. Then ask how they treatment plan is going, are they going to the program if not, inquire as to why. If a client isn't happy with his placement or program, tell the client that you need to talk to the supervisor to see if we can make the situation better. Call the supervisor and make an action plan." If a client is not complying with their program say, 'you need to come in right now.'

My career training helped me to conduct jail interviews with a fair degree of sufficiency however I did not feel particularly well suited for doing casework. It was one of the hardest jobs I have ever held. Accordingly, I had tremendous respect for the strength, compassion and insight that pretrial release workers showed towards the people that they encountered every day.

Managing Career Dilemmas

During my field studies, I was required to negotiate roles and expectations with a range of different people, settings, and organizational agendas. The research was complicated at various points by the political nature of the criminal justice system and its actors. One director would not allow me to begin my research until they had finished revamping the new client database thinking that I might share its components to the other agencies. Another supervisor asked if I was conducting a program evaluation and some line staff asked if I was hired by management to overhaul the inefficiencies in their organization. I believe, for these reasons, that the programs initially expressed a slight reluctance to allow me fully into their organizations. I encountered a number of dilemmas during the course of this research and I employed techniques for managing them in the most ethical manner possible.

Going Off the Record

I pursued interviews with bail commissioners and judges to help me understand how criminal deviance is constructed in the corridors of power. Interviewing judicial officials was important because they played a critical role in making pretrial release decisions. The difficulty I encountered was that some judges were reluctant to give me permission to tape record the interviews. Traditionally, judicial chambers are a personal and less formal environment for discussing criminal cases, and I thought it would be an ideal place to conduct the interview. I first encountered judges' resistance to tape recording when I scheduled an interview with then Bail Commissioner Linda Delaney. During our initial phone conversation, I asked Commissioner Delaney if I could record the interview. There was a long silence before she said, "It depends on the questions." I described the interview guide and she responded noncommittally, "Well, bring it and we'll see." When I arrived at her chambers, I asked her again if I could use the tape recorder, explaining that it would help me to accurately represent her responses. She hesitated and said, "It depends on what you want to know." I reached in my file folder and handed her my interview guide. She glanced over the questions and began to answer them without ever addressing my request. Feeling as if I had lost control of the interview and stripped of my "technological tools," I fumbled for a pen and paper to write down her answers. I limited my note taking to essential words or phrases. I then reconstructed the interview conversation immediately afterward. I thought my interview with Judge Delaney was an anomaly, but I experienced several more failed attempts to tape record my interviews with judges. I completed ten unrecorded interviews with judges and tape recorded two. During the two recorded interviews, one judge asked me to shut off the tape recorder during various parts of the interview, and one judge said that he would deny certain statements if asked about it outside of the interview. I realized that to solicit more open responses from judges, I needed to actively disengage from formal methods for collecting data. Most importantly, I learned a great deal about judge's relationships with pretrial release programs during these "off the record" discussions.

It is worth noting that the political nature of making release decisions may have informed my degree of informational access to court officials. When I was doing field work at the Reach program for example two of the bail commissioners were running for higher office. Perhaps they were less willing to discuss their judging strategies 'on the record' during their electoral campaigns.

Seeking an Exemption

Reducing risk is a primary concern among pretrial release caseworkers and correctional staff in the jail's processing center. Yet I was surprised to learn that caseworkers had authority to traffic inmates in and out of their cells to conduct interviews. At the beginning of the shift, caseworkers identify inmates who are eligible for pretrial release, take them out of the cell to conduct an interview in a small office, and escort them back to the cell once the interview is completed. One afternoon, Kyra Willis, a caseworker for the Reach Program, taught me how to "pull inmates" for interviews. Lt. Davison, a sheriff's deputy, strode toward us and promptly gave me an "on the spot safety lesson" from a correctional perspective. In rapid succession, he taught me to "never leave the tank door open, to keep your foot pressed against the heavy steel door in case an inmate decides to charge and never, ever, step inside [the cell]." I nodded and thanked him for the advice. In parting, he emphasized one last point, "Always keep the keys on your person or hidden from sight. If an inmate gets a hold of them, you will be held responsible." Kyra then handed me the keys and said, "You have about six interviews to do." She walked away. Up to that point, I had embraced all of the opportunities to participate in pretrial release practices. However, I felt apprehensive about taking part in what might be a potentially dangerous task. I approached Kyra and explained that having unsupervised control over inmates in the jail violated the terms of my human subjects review. In truth, there was no specific clause in my IRB proposal, but protocols for ethical social research discourage participation in activities that threaten the safety or reputation of subjects. Kyra appeared confused by my explanation. In hindsight, I should not have used the IRB as an excuse for why I could not participate in pulling inmates. I decided to admit to Kyra that I did not believe that I had enough experience to bear that level of responsibility. She became immediately sympathetic toward my discomfort. She said to me, "I didn't think about how hard it would be for someone new." We were able to negotiate a new division of labor: she "pulled inmates" and I conducted the interviews. This dilemma was also helpful for revealing some interesting findings about jail work. The job of pulling inmates revealed to me that caseworkers play a tremendously important role in the physical management of the jail population. This is true in spite of the fact that caseworkers receive no formal training from the sheriff's department nor are they equipped with any mechanisms of self-defense (i.e., guns, baton, or pepper spray). However, caseworkers benefit from being able to traffic inmates in and out of their cells because it allows them to process cases more quickly and efficiently. They would, alternatively, have to wait for a deputy to escort each inmate to and from the interview room. Caseworkers and deputies share in this responsibility to carry out pretrial release practices in the most resourceful manner possible.

Claiming Expertise

I was drawn into organizational disputes and called on to take sides during my fieldwork. Although at times my researcher status was a detriment for fitting in at the nonprofit agencies, caseworkers and supervisors also sought out my advice on organizational problems. Staffers asked me to comment on their operations since I had worked with other pretrial release agencies and they thought I could offer them a comparative perspective about what works and what does not work in these types of programs. At the Open Door, I was increasingly asked to comment on the interoffice strife. Many people in the agency pointed out that I could be "more objective." Many caseworkers began to seek me out to listen and advise them on the problems the agency faced. Wayne and the supervisory staff wanted to "tap my expertise" on how to make the organization more efficient and get staff to "work smarter." Both sides approached me to develop recommendations to help the agency overhaul its internal structure. I agreed to write up recommendations for improving the agency's daily operation based on my experiences, observations, and discussions with both caseworkers and supervisors. I framed my recommendations as addressing organizational-level problems that might be remedied with structural solutions, such as changing how the court refers defendants and hiring a human resources manager to standardize personnel policies. I did not comment on any interpersonal disagreements between individual staff and supervisory members. Overall, my report was well received by members of the Open Door. Given my status as an unpaid caseworker, I had some authority to speak about the hardships of the job. This meant that my evaluation of agency problems was anchored in real experience, not just bureaucratic observation.

Career Exit

I exited the field site in 2004. During my last week at Reach, Stacy, among others, joked that I should be "arrested" and booked into the county jail, dressed in orange and put in the holding cell "to get a flavor for life on the inside." I politely declined. I was not quite prepared to take my career in that direction. I conducted this research using ethnographic tools because I wanted to see how the law worked in everyday practice at the San Miguel courthouse. I examined up close the varied interactional dynamics that constitute decision making practices when justice is outsourced to the private sector.

Leaving the field is a challenging task and, at times, an emotional decision. For me, I felt the pull to stay longer and the readiness to move on. I think it is a common tension that is generated by a fear that you might be missing something important. During my pretrial release career as an ethnographer, I confronted cultural, bureaucratic and legal barriers as well as opportunities to record critical aspects of lawmaking in the courthouse community. I also found ways to facilitate rapport with my informants without compromising the integrity of the research design. My career dilemmas highlight how an ethnographic study of multiple organizational settings requires a continuous process of negotiation that often transcends the day-to-day mechanics of the methodology itself. One of the greatest lessons that I learned from this fieldwork was how to participate in the social worlds of the people under study and remain a compassionate observer.

References

Albonetti, Celesta A. 1986. "Criminality, Prosecutorial Screening, and Uncertainty: Toward a Theory of Discretionary Decision Making in Felony Case Processings," *Criminology* 24: 623-644.

Albonetti, Celesta and John Hepburn. 1996. "Prosecutorial Discretion to Defer Criminalization: The Effects of Defendant's Ascribed and Achieved Status Characteristics," *Journal of Quantitative Criminology* 12: 63-80.

Allen, Francis A. 1959. "Legal Values and the Rehabilitative Ideal," *Journal of Criminal Law, Criminology, and Police Science* 50: 226-232.

American Friends Service Committee (AFSC). 1971. *Struggle for Justice*. New York: Hall and Wang.

Ares, Charles E., Anne Rankin, and Herbert Sturz. 1963. "The Manhattan Bail Project: An Interim Report on the Use of Pretrial-trial Parole," *New York University Law Review* 38: 67-95.

Austin, James, Barry Krisberg, and Paul Litsky. 1985. "The Effectiveness of Supervised Pretrial Release," *Crime and Delinquency* 31(4): 519-537.

Backer, Thomas. 2005. *Blueprint for Building Evidence-Based Community Partnerships in Corrections*. Northridge, CA: Human Interaction Research Institute.

Beeley, Arthur L. [1927] 1966. *The Bail System in Chicago*. Chicago: University of Chicago Press.

Best, Joel. 1999. *Random Violence: How We Talk About New Crime and New Victims*. Berkeley: University of California Press.

Biggart, Nicole. 1989. *Charismatic Capitalism: Direct Selling Organizations in America*. Chicago: University of Chicago Press.

Blumberg, Abraham. 1967a. "The Practice of Law as a Confidence Game: Organizational Cooptation of a Profession," *Law & Society Review* 1(2): 15-40.

_____.1967b. *Criminal Justice*. Chicago, IL: Quadrangle Books.

Bonnie, Richard H. and John Monohan. 2005. "From Coercion to Contract: Reframing the Debate on Mandated Community Treatment for People with Mental Disorders," *Law and Human Behavior* 29: 485-503.

Boris, Elizabeth and Eugene Steuerle. 2006. *Nonprofits and Government: Collaboration and Conflict*. 2nd ed. Washington, D.C.: Urban Institute Press.

Bridges, George S. and Sara Steen. 1998. "Racial Disparities in Official Assessments Of Juvenile Offenders: Attributional Stereotypes as Mediating Mechanisms," *American Sociological Review* 63: 554-570.

Brinkerhoff, Jennifer M. 2002. "Government-Nonprofit Partnerships: A Defining Framework," *Public Administration and Development* 22: 19-30.

Burns, Stacy and Mark Peyrot. 2003. "Tough love: Nurturing and Coercing Responsibility and Recovery in California Drug Courts," *Social Problems* 50: 416-38.

_____.2008. "Reclaiming Discretion: Judicial Sanctioning Strategy in Court-Supervised Drug Treatment," *Journal of Contemporary Ethnography* 37: 720-744.

Caputo, Gail A. 2004. *Intermediate Sanctions in Corrections*. Denton: University of North Texas Press.

Castellano, Ursula. In Press. "Courting Compliance: Case Mangers as Double Agents in Mental Health Courts," *Law & Social Inquiry*.

Castellano, Ursula. 2007. "Becoming a Non-Expert and Other Strategies for Managing Fieldwork Dilemmas in the Criminal Justice System," Journal *of Contemporary Ethnography* 36 (6): 704-730.

Cicourel, Aaron Victor. 1995. *The Social Organization of Juvenile Justice*. New Brunswick, NJ: Transaction Books.

Conley, John M. and William M. O'Barr. 1990. *Rules Versus Relationships: The Ethnography of Legal Discourse*. Chicago: University of Chicago Press.

Conley, John M., William M. O'Barr and E. Allan Lind. 1978. "Power of Language:
Presentation Style in the Courtroom," *Duke Law Journal* 78: 1375-99.

Coston, J. M. 1998. "A Model and Typology of Government-NGO Partnerships," *Nonprofit and Voluntary Sector Quarterly* 27(3): 358-382.

Coutin, Susan Bibler. 2000. *Legalizing Moves: Salvadoran Immigrants' Struggle for U.S. Residency*. Ann Arbor: University of Michigan Press.

Crawford, Adam. 2003. "Contractual Governance of Deviant Behavior," *Journal of Law and Society* 30(4): 479-505.

Davis, Angela. 2007. *Arbitrary Justice: The Power of the American Prosecutor*. New York: Oxford University Press,

DeHoog, R. H. 1990. "Competition, Negotiation or Cooperation: Three Models of Service Contracting," *Administration and Society* 22(3): 317-340.

Demuth, Stephen. 2003. "Racial and Ethnic Differences in Pretrial Release Decisions and Outcomes: A Comparison of Hispanic, Black and White Felony Arrestees," *Criminology* 41(3): 873-907.

Dill, Forrest. 1972. *Bail and Bail Reform: A Sociological Study*. Ph.D. dissertation, University of California, Berkeley.

Dixon, Jo. 1995. "The Organizational Context of Criminal Sentencing," *American Journal of Sociology* 100(5): 1157-1198.

Eisenstein, James and Herbert Jacob. 1977. *Felony Justice: An Organizational Analysis of the Criminal Courts*. Boston and Toronto: Little, Brown and Company.

Eisenstein, James, Roy Flemming, and Peter Nardulli. 1988. *The Contours of Justice: Communities and Their Courts*. Boston: Little, Brown.

Emerson, Robert M. 1969. *Judging Delinquents: Context and Process in Juvenile Court*. Chicago: Aldine Press.

_____.1991. "Case processing and Interorganizational Knowledge: Detecting the 'Real Reasons' for Referrals," *Social Problems* 38: 198-212.

Emerson, Robert M. and Sheldon L. Messinger. 1977. "The Micro-Politics of Trouble," *Social Problems* 25(2): 121-134.

Emerson, Robert and Blair Paley. 1992. "Organizational Horizons and Compliant-Filing," Pp 231-47 in *The Uses of Discretion*, edited by K. Hawkins. New York: Oxford University Press.

Emmelman, Debra. 2003. *Justice for the Poor: A Study of Criminal Defense Work*. Burlington, VT: Ashgate.

Feeley, Malcolm M. 1979. *The Process is the Punishment: Handling Cases in the Lower Criminal Courts*. New York: Russell Sage Foundation.

Feeley, Malcolm M. and Jonathan Simon. 1992. "The New Penology: Notes on the Emerging Strategy of Corrections and Its Implications," *Criminology* 30(4): 449–474.

Flemming, Roy. 1982. *Punishment Before Trial: An Organizational Perspective of Felony Bail Processes*. New York: Longman.

Flemming, Roy, Peter Nardulli, and James Eisenstein. 1993. *The Craft of Justice: Work and Politics in Criminal Court Communities*. Philadelphia: University of Pennsylvania Press.

Foote, Caleb. 1954. "Compelling Appearance in Court: Administration of Bail in Philadelphia," *University of Pennsylvania Law Review* 102: 1031-1079.

Foucault, Michel. 1979. *Discipline and Punish: The Birth of the Prison*. (Translation:Alan Sheridan). New York: Vintage Books.

Fox, Kathryn. 2005. "Coercing Change: How Institutions Induce Correction in the Culture of Self-Change," Pp 105-120 in *Sociology of Crime, Law and Deviance, Vol. 6: Ethnographies of Law and Social Control*, edited by Stacy Burns. Boston: Elsevier JAI.

Frazier, Charles, E. Wilbur Bock and John C. Henretta. 1980. "Pretrial Release and Bail Decisions: The Effects of Legal, Community, and Personal Variables," *Criminology* 18: 162-181.

French, J and B. H. Raven. 1959. "The Bases of Social Power," Pp 50-67 in *Studies in Social Power,* edited by Dorwin Cartwright. Ann Arbor: Institute for Social Research, University of Michigan.

Frohmann, Lisa. 1991. "Discrediting Victims' Allegations of Sexual Assault: Prosecutorial Accounts of Case Rejections," *Social Problems* 38: 213-226.

Garland, David. 2001. *The Culture of Control: Crime and Social Order in Contemporary Society*. New York: Oxford University Press.

Glendon, Mary Ann. 1994. *A Nation Under Lawyers: How the Crisis in the Legal Profession is transforming American Society*. New York: Farrar, Straus and Giroux.

Goffman, Erving. 1959. *The Presentation of Self.* New York: Harper.

_____.1961. *Asylums: Essays on the Social Situation of Mental Patients and Other Defendants*. Garden City, NY: Anchor books.

_____.1974. *Frame Analysis: An Essay on the Organization of Experience.* New York: Harper.

Goldfarb, Ronald. 1965. *Ransom: A Critique of the American Bail System*. New York: Harper & Row.

Goldkamp, John S. 1979. *Two Classes of Accused: A Study of Bail and Detention in American Justice*. Cambridge, MA: Ballinger.

Gottfredson, Michael R. and Don M. Gottfredson. 1988. *Decision Making in Criminal Justice*. 2^d ed. New York, NY: Plenum.

Gubrium, Jaber and James A. Holstein, eds. 2001. *Institutional Selves: Troubled Identities in a Postmodern World*. New York: Oxford University Press.

Haas J. and W. Shaffir. 1982. "Taking on the Role of Doctor: A Dramaturgical Analysis of Professionalization," *Symbolic Interaction* 5: 187-203.

Hagan, John, John Dewitt, and Duane Alwin. 1979. "Ceremonial Justice: Crime and Punishment in a Loosely Coupled System," *Social Forces* 58: 506-527.

Halliday, Simon, Nicola Burns, Neil Hutton, Fergus NcNeill, and Cyrus Tata. 2009. "Street-Level Bureaucracy, Inter-professional Relations, and Coping Mechanisms: A Study of Criminal Justice Social Workers in the Sentencing Process," *Law & Policy* 31(4): 305-329.

Hasenfeld, Yeheskel. 1972. "People Processing Organizations: An Exchange Approach," *American Sociological Review* 37: 256-63.

Hewitt, John and Randall Stokes. 1975. "Disclaimers," *American Sociological Review* 40: 1-11.

Hochschild, Arlie. 1983. *The Managed Heart.* Berkeley: University of California Press.

Holstein, James A. 1992. "Producing People: Descriptive Practice in Human Service Work," Pp 23-40 in *Current Research on Occupations and Professions*, edited by Gale Miller. Greenwich, CT: JAI Press.

Hora, Peggy Fulton, William G. Schema and John T.A. Rosenthal. 1999. "Therapeutic Jurisprudence and the Drug Treatment Court Movement: Revolutionalizing the Criminal Justice System's Response to Drug Treatment Court Movement in America," *Notre Dame Law Review* 74 (January): 439-538.

Ibarra, Peter R. 2005. "Red Flags and Trigger Control: the Role of Human Supervision in an Electronic Monitoring Program," Pp. 31–48 in *Sociology of Crime, Law and Deviance, Vol. 6: Ethnographies of Law and Social Control*, edited by Stacy Lee Burns. Boston: Elsevier JAI.

Irwin, John. 1985. *The Jail: Managing the Underclass in American Society.* Berkeley: University of California Press.

Jacobs, Mark D. 1990. *Screwing the System and Making it Work: Juvenile Justice in the No Fault Society.* Chicago and London: University of Chicago Press.

Jurik, Nancy, Joel Blumenthal, Brian Smith and Edwardo Portillos. 2000. "Organizational Cooptation or Social Change? A Critical Perspective on Community Criminal Justice Partnerships," *Journal of Contemporary Criminal Justice* 16(3): 293-320.

Kelling, George L. and Catherine M. Coles. 1996. *Fixing Broken Windows: Restoring Order and Reducing Crime in Our Communities.* New York: Touchstone Press.

Kleinman, Sheryl. 1996. *Opposing Ambitions: Gender and Identity in an Alternative Organization.* Chicago: University of Chicago Press.

LaFree, Gary D. 1985. "Official Reaction to Hispanic Defendants in the Southwest," *Journal of Research in Crime and Delinquency* 22: 213-237.

Levi, Judith N. 1990. "The Study of Language in the Judicial Process," Pp 9-35 in *Language in the Judicial Process*, edited by Judith N. Levi and Anne Graffam Walker. New York: Plenum Press.

Licherman, Paul. 1989. "Making a Politics of Masculinity," *Comparative Social Research.* 11: 185-208.

Lidz, Charles W. and Andrew W. Walker. 1977. "Therapeutic Control of Heroin: Dedifferentiating Legal and Psychiatric Controls," *Sociological Inquiry* 47: 294-321.

Lipetz, Marcia J. 1984. *Routine Justice: Processing Cases in Women's Court*. New Brunswick and London: Transactions Books.

Lipsky, Michael. 1980. *Street-level Bureaucracy: Dilemmas of the Individual in Public Services*. New York: Russell Sage Foundation.

Loseke, Donileen R. 1992. *The Battered Woman and Shelters*. Albany: SUNY Press.

_____. 2003. *Thinking About Social Problems*, 2nd ed. Hawthorne, NY: Aldine De Gruyter.

Mackinem, Mitchell B. and Paul Higgins. 2007. "Tell Me About the Test: The Construction of Truth and Lies in Drug Court," *Journal of Contemporary Ethnography* 36(3): 223-251.

Margolin, Leslie. 1997. *Under the Cover of Kindness: The Invention of Social Work*. Charlotte and London: University Press of Virginia.

Maynard, Douglas. 1984. *Inside Plea Bargaining: The Language of Negotiation*. New York and London: Plenum Press.

McConville, Mike, Andrew Sanders, and Roger Leng. 1991. *The Case for the Prosecution*. London and New York: Routledge.

Melossi, Dario. 1990. *The State Of Social Control: A Sociological Study of Concepts Of State and Social Control in the Making of Democracy*. New York: St. Martin's Press.

Merry, Sally Engle. 1990. *Getting Justice, Getting Even: Legal Consciousness Among Working-Class Americans*. Chicago: University of Chicago Press.

Mileski, Maureen. 1971. "Courtroom Encounters: An Observational Study of a Lower Criminal Court," *Law & Society Review* 5: 473-538.

Miller, Gale. 1991. *Enforcing the Work Ethic: Rhetoric and Everyday Life in a Work Incentive Program*. Albany: SUNY Press.

Miller JoAnn and Donald C. Johnson. 2009. *Problem Solving Courts: New Approaches to Criminal Justice*. Lanham: Rowman and Littlefield Publishers.

Munetz, Mark and Jennifer Teller. 2003. "The Challenges of Cross-Disciplinary Collaborations: Bridging the Mental Health and Criminal Justice Systems," *Capital Law Review* 32: 935-950.

Murphy, John J. 1971. "Revision of State Bail Laws," *Ohio State Law Journal* 32: 451- 485.

Nadar, Laura. 1969. "Up The Anthropologist-Perspectives Gained From Studying Up," Pp 97–116 in *Reinventing Anthropology*, edited by D. Hymes. New York: Vintage Books.

Nolan, James L. Jr. 2001. *Reinventing Justice: The American Drug Court Movement*. Princeton and Oxford: Princeton University Press.

Paik, Leslie. 2006. "Are You Truly a Recovering Dope Fiend? Local Interpretative Practices at a Therapeutic Community Drug Treatment Program," *Symbolic Interaction* 29(2): 213-234.

_____. 2009. "Maybe He's Depressed: Mental Illness as a Mitigating Factor for Drug Offender Accountability," *Law & Social Inquiry* 34(3): 569–602.

Peete, Thomas. 1993. "Recommended For Release on Recognizance: Factors Affecting Pretrial Release Recommendations," *Journal of Social Psychology* 134(3): 375-382.

Peyrot, Mark. 1985. "Coerced Voluntarism: The Micro-Politics of Drug Treatment," *Urban Life* 13: 343-65.

Pretrial Justice Institute. 2009. *Survey of Pretrial Services Programs.* WashingtonD.C.:
http://www.pretrial.org/Docs/Documents/PJI%27s%20Survey%20of%20Pr
etrial%20Programs%202009.2.pdf (accessed November 19th, 2010).

Redlich, Allison. 2005. "Voluntary, but Knowing and Intelligent: Comprehension in Mental Health Courts," *Psychology, Public Policy, and the Law* 11: 605-619.

Reich, Jennifer A. 2005. *Fixing Families: Parents, Power, and the Child Welfare System.* New York: Routledge.

Roman, Caterina, Gretchen Moore, Susan Jenkins, and Kevonne Small. 2002. *Understanding Community Justice Partnerships: Assessing the Capacity to Partner.* Washington D.C.: Urban Institute.

Salamon, Lester M. 1987. "Partners in Public Service: The Scope and Theory of Government-Nonprofit Relations," Pp 99-177 in *The Non-profit Sector,* edited by Walter Powell. New Haven and London: Yale University Press.

Salamon, Lester. 2002. *The Tools of Government: A Guide to the New Governance.* New York: Oxford University Press.

Savelsberg, Joachim J. 1992. "Law That Does Not Fit Society: Sentencing Guidelines as a Neoclassical Reaction to the Dilemmas of Substantivized Law," *American Journal of Sociology* 97(5): 1346-1381.

Scott, Marvin B. and Stanford Lyman. 1968. "Accounts," *American Sociological Review* 33: 1268-1275.

Seligson, Susan Berk. 2002. *The Bilingual Courtroom: The Role of the Court Interpreter in the Judicial Process.* Chicago: University Of Chicago Press.

Sherwood-Fabre, Liese. 1987. "An Evaluation of Federal Pretrial Release Services Agencies' Impact on Pretrial Decisions and Outcomes," *Evaluation Review* 11(1): 3-31.

Silverstein, Martin. 2001. "Ties that Bind: Family Surveillance of Canadian Parolees," *The Sociological Quarterly* 42(3): 395-420

Smith, Steven R. and Michael Lipsky. 1993. *Nonprofits for Hire: The Welfare State in the Age of Contracting.* Cambridge: Harvard University Press.

Snow, David, Susan G. Baker, and Leon Anderson. 1989. "Criminality and Homeless Men: An Empirical Assessment," *Social Problems* 36(5): 532-549.

Sudnow, David. 1965. "Normal Crimes: Sociological Features of the Penal Code in the Public Defender's Office," *Social Problems* 12(3): 255-276.

Thomas, Wayne H. 1976. *Bail Reform in America.* Berkeley and Los Angeles: University of California Press.

Ulmer, Jeffery M. and John H. Kramer. 1996. "Court Communities under Sentencing Guidelines: Dilemmas of Formal Rationality and Sentencing Disparity," *Criminology* 34(3): 383-405.

Ulmer, Jeffrey. 1997. *Social Worlds of Sentencing: Court Communities Under Sentencing Guidelines.* Albany: SUNY.

Uphoff, Rodney, J. 1992. "The Criminal Defense Lawyer: Zealous Advocate, Double Agent, or Beleaguered Dealer?" *Criminal Law Bulletin* 28(5): 419-456.

Walker, Samuel. 1993. *Taming the System: The Control of Discretion in Criminal Justice, 1950-1990.* New York: Oxford University Press.

_____. 2001. *Sense and Nonsense About Crime and Drugs.* 5th ed. Belmont, CA: Wadsworth.

Weber, Max. 1952. *The Protestant Ethic and the Spirit of Capitalism*. New York: Scribner.

Weber, Max [1924] 1968. *Economy and Society: An Outline of Interpretive Sociology*, edited by Guenther Roth and Claus Wittich. New York: Bedminister Press.

Welsh, Wayne N. 1995. *Counties in Court: Jail Overcrowding and Court-Ordered Reform*. Philadelphia: Temple University Press.

Whiteacre, Kevin W. 2007. "Strange Bedfellows: The Tensions of Coerced Treatment," *Criminal Justice Policy Review* 18(3): 260-273

Wice, Paul B. 1974. *Freedom for Sale: A National Study of Pretrial Release*. Toronto and London: Lexington Books.

Young, Dennis R. 2000. "Alternative Models Of Government-Nonprofit Sector Relations: Theoretical and International Perspectives," *Nonprofit and Voluntary Sector Quarterly* 29: 149-172.

Yngvesson, Barbara. 1989. "Inventing Law in Local Settings: Rethinking Popular Legal Culture," *The Yale Law Journal* 98: 1689-1709.

Index

About the Book

Do pretrial release programs, initiated and now operated by a range of nonprofit organizations to redress the inequalities of the bail system, affect the administration of justice? Specifically, do they lessen the barriers to justice often faced by poor and minority defendants? Ursula Castellano's ethnographic study of three pretrial release programs reveals the often unintended consequences of incorporating social service nonprofits in the criminal court process.

Castellano explores the intimate workings of pretrial release programs to show how contract caseworkers now play a critical role at nearly every stage of the criminal justice process—and also how well-intentioned nonprofits can end up compromising the traditional adversarial legal process in the name of treatment, sometimes in ways that are detrimental for defendants. In the process, she raises new questions about the increasing involvement of nonprofits in the operation of government.

Ursula Castellano is assistant professor of sociology and anthropology at Ohio University.